WANTED: FIRST CHILD

Wanted:
First Child

A Birth Mother's Story

REBECCA HARSIN

FITHIAN PRESS · SANTA BARBARA · 1991

Design and typography by Jim Cook
Cover photograph courtesy of Cottage Hospital of Santa Barbara

LIBRARY OF CONGRESS CATALOGING-IN-PUBLICATION DATA
Harsin, Rebecca, 1952-
    Wanted—first child / Rebecca Harsin.
      p.   cm.
    ISBN 0-931832-69-1
    1. Adoption—United States—Case studies. 2. Birthparents—
United States—Case studies. 3. Adoptees—United States—Case
studies. I. Title.
HV875.55.H37   1990
362.7′34′0973—DC20
                                                    90-13887
                                                       CIP

To Jennifer

A loss is only a loss when it can never be found again. My love for you allowed me never to give up what I thought I had lost forever.

I WAS NINE YEARS OLD, sitting on our back porch steps watching our mother cat circling her five baby kittens. She lay down on her side to let them nurse. I was feeling very maternal that day.

From that point on, I wasn't thinking of being a nurse, a stewardess or a teacher, I was thinking of being a mother. I played "house" all the time. My dolls were some of the cleanest, best dressed dolls in town. I practiced my love and patience on my dolls. For me, being a mother was my goal in life. By the age of twelve I had forgotten about playing with dolls. I was busy being a cheerleader and flirting with the boys. Life seemed so simple then.

I grew up in a very small town where everyone knew everyone and everyone knew what the others were doing at all times. Not knowing how the other half lived, I was very secure and content to be like the other women in town. They married young, had babies when they were young, and helped their husbands with the farming. I just knew I was going to marry my first love. We had been going together since I was thirteen. We had talked a lot about how many children we wanted, and six is what we settled on.

Until I was fifteen all seemed well in my life. Then one evening I heard my parents arguing. I went to the bottom of the stairs hoping I could hear a little better what was going on. My father seemed angry and my mother was crying. Then it suddenly became quiet. My father had left.

I sat in my room that night wondering what the fight was all about. The next day I learned it had been my parents' final argument before they told us kids that their twenty-year marriage was going to be terminated in divorce court.

I shook for days. My whole world had fallen apart. My mother cried all the time and I couldn't comfort her. My father married the much younger woman he had had an affair with and packed up and moved to another state. I missed my father and the family life as I had known it, but I was beginning to adjust to the fact that Dad wasn't coming home and we would all just go on with our lives—a little sadder, but we would just continue on.

Several months later my mother just couldn't cope with the memories of Dad and the house they shared, or with the talk in town. Her decision was made. The house was sold, we packed up and moved to a large city four hundred miles from home.

Leaving my home and all my friends was just the beginning of all my hurt and confusion.

THE CITY WAS OVER-
whelming to me. Cars everywhere, large buildings, people everywhere, more houses than I had ever seen before. We rented a large
apartment for the first few months until we found the "right"
house.

I still missed my dad. My sister Susan, who is eighteen months
older than myself, had married her boyfriend at the age of seventeen, and they had moved to another state. I now believe she moved
just to get out of the mess our family had been pushed into. I missed
her, too. My older brother Ron, who was with us for a short time
before he went away to college, tried to take on the role of father.
My younger sister Trish, who was with us for about a year, was
asked by my Dad to come live with him and the "other woman."
After she left, my mother and I were alone for awhile.

The school I went to was the largest building I had ever been in.
Getting lost every day and always being the last student to come
into the room was starting to wear down the patience of every
teacher I had. After several months of this, I'd had it. People didn't
know me. I wasn't popular, I wasn't a cheerleader. I missed my
friends back home.

I can look back now and see why my life was so miserable then. I
had built a wall around myself. I walked around with a chip on my
shoulder; I was miserable and unhappy and I was going to make
sure everyone knew it. I never smiled and hardly ever talked to
anyone. I figured if I could make myself the most miserable person
in the world, my mother would see my unhappiness and send me

back home to live with my grandmother or, better yet, with my best friend. That never happened and I finally realized it never would.

I took up with several girls I thought were pretty nice. They didn't live the way I lived; you might say they "came from the other side of the tracks." Smoking and drinking were their favorite pastimes and I joined in. Drinking every other day and getting drunk on the weekends was what I did best. That went on for months until my sophomore year was about to end.

One day my friend Katy brought some pills to school. She said they were tranquilizers and they would make me feel "real good." I took one, and waited. But I felt nothing, so I waited in the hall for Katy. I told her she must be crazy because I didn't feel a thing, so she gave me another one as we were about to go into our next class.

By the time school was out I had taken five of those pills. I don't know how I got home, but the first thing I remember was my mother screaming at me, "What's wrong, what's wrong?" I was sitting on the floor in my bedroom, eyes all glazed over, mumbling something about a pill. My mother ran to phone a friend, who told her, "Make her throw up now!" I remember my head in the toilet bowl and someone else's finger pushing down my throat.

My mother took me to the doctor the next morning. I was scolded unmercifully by the doctor and told how lucky I was to have gotten some of what I had done to myself out of my system when I did. He said I could have done irreversible damage to myself.

I began to wake up to a few facts in life after that episode, and I stopped running around with those friends. I decided just to be by myself, but that didn't last long. A month before my sophomore year was to end, I was approached by a girl named Kellee. She took me aside and told me some secrets about my "old" friends and asked me if I was still running around with them. She told me she had often wondered why I hung around girls like that, for she knew I wasn't part of that crowd. Kellee introduced me to her friends, and soon I was accepted into a new group.

I began feeling better about myself and started being my old self again. I was laughing again, and I was feeling good. I wasn't even thinking as much of my old friends back home, nor did I even want to go back to my small hometown anymore.

The summer before my junior year was a busy one. If I wanted to drive a car and run around, I had to make my own money. I babysat for some neighbors, I cleaned houses for two wealthy women in the neighborhood, and I worked for a neighbor who was an insurance agent working out of his home. I helped him with the filing, and once a week I cleaned his home. I also watched his two children, who didn't want any other babysitter but me.

My junior year started out great. During the summer I had met a lot of new friends. I wasn't sad or unsure of myself anymore, and the very thought of moving back to my old hometown made me shudder inside. I had grown away from the security a small town gives. I had tested my wings and found out that flying was a whole lot more fun than nesting.

I still thought about my old friends and went home to visit them now and again, but each time I returned they seemed different. Or was it I who was different? The town was so small and empty all the time. Each time I left I thought I must have been crazy to have been so upset for leaving this behind.

One thing that hadn't changed was my strong feelings about motherhood. I still thought about a cute little cottage-type home; it didn't have to have a white picket fence, just as long as it had some kind of fence to keep the children inside and away from cars. I hadn't even had any children yet, but I found myself worrying about them already.

Halfway through my junior year I met and fell in love with Greg. We were inseparable. After a date Greg would call me as soon as he got home and we would talk until one of us fell asleep. Everything was right in my world; I was doing well in school and I had good friends, but best of all, I had Greg.

The school year went by quickly, and soon it was summer again. I was still with Greg, but around the middle of May he told me he was leaving soon with several of his friends to work in California for the summer. I dreaded his leaving.

After Greg left, my girlfriends and I started getting back together and doing things again. Most of my time had been spent with Greg; I'd hardly spent any time with them. One Saturday evening in July we went downtown to drive around and see what was "new." It really didn't matter; we were just looking for the guys. Greg was out of sight and out of mind so to speak, and I was sure he was having a great time without me, too. We met three pretty nice-looking guys and they asked us to come over to their place for a drink. We followed them home, where I started talking to one of them, Mike. He was short but cute. I was used to Greg towering over me—he was 6'4" but Mike was only about 5'10".

Mike and I talked for the better part of the evening, and too soon it was time for me to get home. Mike asked for my phone number and I gave it to him. He didn't seem too interested in me that evening, and I really didn't think I would hear from him again; but on the following Sunday afternoon I got a call from him asking me if I would like to go with him for a ride.

We took a drive up to a lake not far from town. We talked non-stop for hours. He told me of his previous girlfriend with whom he had recently broken up. I knew he was still hurting inside. I told him all about Greg. We seemed to understand one another.

When it was getting close to dark I had to be getting home. We said "so long," and I still thought we wouldn't see each other again. But Mike called the next morning and asked if I would go out to dinner with him that evening. We had a nice dinner and I really enjoyed myself being with Mike.

After several weeks of seeing each other every day or night I found myself thinking less about Greg and more about Mike. Greg would write to me almost every day and I would write back almost as often. Never would I tell him about Mike, and I hoped he would never find out.

One hot August Saturday afternoon Mike called me and asked if I would come over. He said he wanted to talk to me, and I heard an urgency in his voice. I immediately went over to his home and he sat me down and told me he had been drafted. He said he was going into the Marines and would be leaving soon for boot-camp. I felt sad for Mike: he was going to become involved with the Viet Nam War.

We spent as much time together as we could until the Saturday before Mike left for bootcamp. Mike asked me if I would spend Saturday night with him and stay with him until he had to leave for bootcamp. I called my mother and told her I was going to stay with Mike until he left on Monday. Mom argued with me and told me to come home and that I had no business spending the night with Mike. I told her not to worry about me and that I would call her the next morning. That night we cried together, we held each other and we made love. This was our bond together, our way of saying goodbye.

Monday morning came too fast, and we were at the airport saying goodbye. When the plane took off, I knew I was going to miss him.

School soon started again; it was my senior year. For the first month everything seemed to be going fine. Mike wrote as often as he could and told me all about his training.

One morning I woke up with the queasiest stomach I had ever had. I went into the bathroom and threw up. The same thing happened the next several mornings, and then I realized I had missed my period. This just couldn't be. I made all sorts of excuses for my condition. It was the flu, I told myself, or I was stressed out about something at school. It just couldn't be that I was pregnant.

I dreaded telling my mother, but I had to. She was very upset and we both cried. We decided not to talk about it anymore until I had seen a doctor. Several days passed, and I found myself sitting in the doctor's office. He would call me with the results, he said. I waited for the call. It came, and I was.

At first I was numb all over. What was I going to do? My mother mentioned abortion, but I looked at her with such hurt in my eyes that this option was never mentioned again.

Now came the hard part. I had to tell my grandmother, who had moved to our city several years after we had moved to be closer to us. Grandma was the pillar of the family. When any of us was in trouble we always called on Grandma. Here it was. Grandma was sitting in our living room not knowing what I was about to tell her. Finally, I gathered my courage and told her I was pregnant. Grandma stood up quickly and glared at me with hate in her eyes. She started to cry, which was something Grandma just never did; I never saw her cry even when Grandpa died. I went to put my arms around her, but she shoved me aside and told me to get away from her. She hurried out the front door so fast I thought she might fall down the steps. I grabbed her arm to make sure she didn't fall, but once she was safely down the steps she pushed me away again. That was the last time I saw or talked to her for many months.

Mom decided I could stay at home until I started to "show." The plan was then to send me out of the state to a home for unwed mothers. There I would have my baby and give it up for adoption. I agreed to go away to have the baby, but when my mother talked about adoption, I would turn a deaf ear.

Mike and I continued to write regularly. I finally had the courage to write and tell him I was pregnant. Then a week went by with no reply. Finally I received Mike's letter acknowledging that I was pregnant. His letter didn't say much, except that he was sorry.

Sorry, I thought to myself, that's going to help me now. I was hurt and confused and felt that if that was all Mike was going to say about me being pregnant, then I would just leave it at that and be more by myself than I was already.

A couple of days later, Mike called me. He said he had been thinking about me being pregnant, and he asked me what I thought we should do. He said the reason his letter had sounded so distant was that it was quite a shock to him, but he felt badly that I was going through this by myself.

Mike said he was going to ask for a leave so he could come home and we could figure out what we were going to do.

In the last letter I ever wrote to Mike I said I would never ask anything of him, nor did I want him to feel obliged to me or to the baby in any way. This was my way of letting him off the hook. But our letters must have crossed in the mail, for the next day I received a letter from him asking me to marry him. He said he loved me. He would be home in a week, so he said, and we could talk about our marriage plans. At last, I felt some relief. He wanted to marry me and take care of his baby.

When I told my mother about Mike's letter she became angry and told me in no uncertain terms that marriage would never be the answer to my "problem." She became hostile toward Mike and told me I was not to see him or even to talk to him when he came to town on leave. I was not going to marry him and have him leave me a few years down the road because he "had" to marry me. No way was any man going to do that to her daughter. Mother was still feeling the pain of her own divorce, I thought, and decided I'd better not say anything more about it to her.

That evening, my mother came into my room and sat down on the bed next to me. She told me to listen very carefully because this was the way things were going to be. As long as I was a minor and still under her care, she had every right to say how and when and why. She told me not to answer the phone under any circumstances because it might be Mike. Her plan was to tell him that I had been sent to Louisiana to stay with my Uncle Norm. I was no longer at home and he was not to call or come over ever again. He was to go away and leave me alone, and to never darken our doorway again. Mother had put all the blame on Mike. I couldn't believe what I had heard and I truly didn't believe she meant a word of it, nor that it could ever happen that way.

But she meant it. Whenever the phone rang she jumped and raced to answer it. I was in my room one evening doing my homework when the phone rang. My door was closed but I could hear my mother's voice. It sounded strained. I opened my bedroom door to listen, and I heard, "I mean this, Mike, she's gone and we don't ever want to hear from you again." She slammed the phone down. She was pale and looked weak. She sat down in the chair in the living room. I went into the living room and sat down on the couch. She was shaking by then, and I asked her what she had just done.

Mother gritted her teeth and looked at me very angrily. "That was Mike and I told him you were gone. I told him he was not to call here ever again or to have any contact with this family ever again." She told me again that I was not to answer the phone, lest Mike call back and find out she had lied to him.

I just sat there not wanting to believe what I heard. How could she run my life like that? Her face softened as she walked over and sat down on the couch next to me and took my hand. I was crying. She told me she was sorry she had to do it, but she was only trying to protect me from getting into a marriage that would break my heart. Mike would always have felt that he had been forced into marrying me, and he would be bitter and resentful toward me always. Then he would leave me with a child to raise by myself, and it would not be fair to the child to give it a broken home like I had.

I went back to my room. What my mother said to me about Mike feeling trapped and resentful toward me finally sank in. How could I ever marry a man who would feel that way toward me? What if he felt that way toward the baby?

That was it. I had to continue with my mother, her plan, and her lie.

A week passed and I knew Mike should be in town. During the next two days the phone rang almost nonstop. I had promised Mom I would not answer it, and I tried to keep my promise. It kept ringing and ringing and I thought the chances of it being Mike were pretty small, after what Mother had told him. Finally, I picked up the phone.

"Becki, is that you? Becki, don't hang up!" A woman's voice? "Becki, this is Sherry, Mike's sister-in-law. We've been trying for days to reach you. Please tell me what's going on. Mike is here with me now and he's just beside himself. Becki, he loves you, please talk to him."

Mike was on the phone now. "Becki, why is this happening? I need to see you. I can't come to your house, your mother might see me there."

MOTHER was at work and she had the car. I told Mike to come over, she wouldn't be home for several more hours. Mike came over and we sat on the couch and held each other and cried. He was hurt and confused, but I kept remembering my mother's words: "trapped and resentful." I had to stop crying and change my attitude. I had to tell Mike marriage wasn't the answer for us, and that I had to work this out on my own. It hurt me to say the things I said to him; I was hurting him and I was hurting myself.

Soon it was getting so close to the time that Mom came home from work that I told Mike he must go and that I would talk to him tomorrow after Mom left for work.

Mike had just pulled out of the driveway as Mother drove up. Her car screamed up the driveway, and she shot into the house like a crazy woman. I ran into my room. I could hear her talking to someone on the phone. It must be her best friend Vera; she tells her everything. They talked forever, it seemed. Then the talking stopped and my bedroom door slowly opened. Mother came in and stood in the doorway and told me to get my things packed and not to forget all the maternity clothes she had bought me a week ago, because I was growing now and would have to leave my other clothes at home.

"You are going to the Morris's home for unwed mothers in Washington," she said. "Our plane leaves at 3:45 tomorrow afternoon. I will be staying with my friend Carol for a few days until you are settled in at the home. I'll go to the home with you, and Carol will pick me up from there." So it hadn't been Vera she was talking to, but the home for unwed mothers.

I was drained, emotionally confused. I packed my suitcases and called my girlfriends. They were at the airport the next day to say goodbye. I hugged them and told them goodbye. Mom and I walked to the ramp and entered the plane. I sat down in the seat, but no matter how I tried not to embarrass myself the tears just kept coming. No Mike, no friends; just Mom, the baby, and me.

THE PLANE LANDED with quite a thud and startled me out of my daydreaming. I didn't want to think anymore. I didn't want to be here, I knew that.

A woman from the home was at the airport waiting to take me to my new residence. We talked very little as we drove to the home. I didn't feel much like conversation. When we drove up to the building my first thought was how much it looked like the old orphanages one sees in books, with three or four poorly dressed, sad looking children and a caption reading, "These children need a home. Can you help?"

Inside, the home was clean, but old and gloomy. Everything seemed to be brown. I didn't see anyone until we started up the stairs to my bedroom. Several girls were coming down the stairs and they gave me a quick look and a faint smile as they passed. The dormitory was large and clean, and all six beds were neatly made. The woman sat my suitcases on my bed. She told me to unpack and to put my belongings in the top two drawers of the dresser. No one else was in the room, so I put everything away as I was told.

I sat down on the bed. Then I lay down on the bed and curled up into a little ball. I started to cry, but stopped suddenly when someone walked into the room.

"Hi!" she said. "My name's Penny. Mrs. Marting sent me up here to get you. Supper's on."

Penny and I walked down to the "mess hall." The room was full of long, large tables, and there were a lot more girls than I thought there would be.

Mrs. Marting walked over to me and said, "Girls, this is Becki. Will you please introduce yourselves to her."

One by one they gave their first names and quick smiles. I sat down and ate and talked with a few of the girls at my table. "How far along are you, when's your due date, what happened to the father of the baby?" The usual questions, I thought to myself.

After supper we carried our plates and glasses to the kitchen, and Mrs. Marting asked Penny to show me around. First we went to the classroom. It looked like any typical classroom: desks, chalkboard, and a global map. There was an adjoining room full of typewriters. From there we went to the other bedrooms. Each had six beds in it. The bathrooms looked like the kind you see at schools: three toilets, four showerheads on the open wall, four sinks lined up against a wall with four small milky-looking mirrors. Next we visited Mrs. Marting's office, the nurse's office, and the smoking and card room downstairs. This last room became the room I spent most of my time in. It had a large round coffee table, a dozen decks of cards on the table and ash trays overflowing with cigarette butts. Next to this was another table with three chairs, used for writing letters home. There were also two small couches and three small lounging chairs.

When my tour was over, Penny asked me if I'd like to stay in the card room and play some cards. I said sure, and asked her how to play. I had never played cards before, except "Old Maid" way back in my younger days. Penny decided to start me out on "Fish." I caught on to it quickly and we played for about two hours.

At nine-thirty in the evening Penny said we had to get upstairs and get ready for bed; "lights out" was at ten. This was going to take a while to get used to; I hadn't been told to go to bed at a certain time in years. But I was tired that night, so I decided I'd grumble tomorrow about going to bed at ten.

I was in the bathroom brushing my teeth when Mrs. Marting walked in.

"Becki," she said, "in the morning at nine-thirty, Miss Miller (the woman who picked me up at the airport) is going to take you to our clinic so our doctor can give you a checkup and you'll need to get your blood work done, too. Please be ready around nine.

Goodnight; I'll see you tomorrow around noon, then I'll take you downstairs and introduce you to our teacher."

I crawled into bed and lay my head down on a pillow that was hard and old-smelling. I wished I had my foam rubber pillow from home. I lay there quite awhile before the tears and sobbing came, and they went on most of the night. Why couldn't I just shut up? I didn't cry in front of other people like that, why was I doing it now? I finally drifted off to sleep.

The next morning I awoke with a start. The first thing my eyes saw was a room that wasn't familiar to me. It all sunk in pretty fast.

Penny came over and sat down on my bed. "Pretty rough night, huh?"

"Yeah," I said.

"Well, I'll tell you, Becki, we've all been through that first night. It makes you feel real bad when you hear someone cry like that, but it must be a built-in instinct to just let you cry and get it all out of your system. The girls who feel like they should comfort the ones crying know they really can't do them any favors. The girls who get comforted by someone else just cry night after night; the ones who don't get any comfort from the others just get all the crying out of them that first night, and it seems to be easier on everybody."

I slowly got out of bed and walked to the bathroom. I took my shower and got dressed. It was already eight; breakfast was at seven-thirty. I walked down to the mess hall anyway to see if there was any breakfast left, but when I walked in, the last two girls were just putting their plates in the kitchen. I was hungry but I guessed I could wait until noon.

I started to walk out with the other two girls when Mrs. Tibbs, the cook, snorted, "Hey you, young lady, get back in here." I turned around slowly and started walking toward her.

"I don't know your name yet, and I didn't see your face at the breakfast table, so where do you think you're going?"

"I thought I'd have to wait until noon to eat because I was late this morning," I said.

"Oh, you thought that now, did you?" she said. "One thing I don't let my girls do is go hungry. Now sit down and I'll fix you a bowl of cold cereal and some juice."

I liked Mrs. Tibbs right off. We talked a little as she cleaned off the tables and straightened the chairs.

When I was done with my cereal and juice, I took my dishes into the kitchen. I thanked Mrs. Tibbs, and she told me to come with her; she had something she wanted to show me.

"I've had five kids myself and during my pregnancies I was always hungry, so if you ever find yourself hungry or you just want a snack, here it is."

Mrs. Tibbs opened a large cupboard in the corner of the kitchen. It was a food addict's dream-come-true! Snow-balls, Hostess cup-cakes, Twinkies, candy bars, peanuts, crackers, marshmallows, and pop.

"I always keep this well-stocked. I know it's all junk, but we all know what we're like when we're pregnant." I gave her a great big smile and she scooted me out of the kitchen and told me to get going, she had to start preparing lunch.

I went straight to Mrs. Marting's office to wait for Miss Miller. Miss Miller came in short of breath and told me she was sorry she was late, but she had to run one of the girls over to the hospital. Her water had broken around 7:45 this morning and she had to stay and get her checked in and fill out all the paper work.

"Well Becki, let's get going, we don't want to be late," Miss Miller said.

As we stepped outside the cold air took my breath away. It was the middle of January, and much colder here than at home. I pulled my coat tightly around my tummy; can't let the baby get cold, I thought.

The clinic wasn't too far away. I was handed a sheet of paper to fill out, then I was called into one of the rooms where a young woman in her early twenties told me she was going to take a little blood. She checked both arms for a good-looking vein and chose my left arm.

I HAD hated needles and shots since childhood. With only one doctor and one nurse in our little town, we had to take what we got. Every time I had to have a shot that one nurse always gave it, and she never was gentle. She'd rub my arm or bottom with the cold alcohol until I knew she had rubbed the skin off, and then she would jab that needle into me with such force that I knew the whole syringe had just been implanted into my body.

Here came the needle. I closed my eyes, it would all be over in a second. Wrong!

"I'm sorry," the young woman said, "I didn't hit the vein; I'll have to do it again."

The second time she didn't do it right, either. Now a third poke, and a fourth poke. I broke out in a cold sweat, and I could feel myself getting faint. "Are you all right?" she asked. She was shaking too, now, and was quite upset.

"No," I said, "will you please get someone else?" My sentence was interrupted by someone walking into the room.

"I'll take that," she snapped. The young woman left the room. An older woman, in her fifties, I guessed, quite attractive but stern looking, picked up my arm and looked at it. "I'm so sorry," she said, "there's no excuse for this." She took the needle, finished the job without my feeling a thing.

"The doctor will be with you shortly," she said. "Please undress and sit on the table."

Then the doctor came in. He was short and stocky and had gray hair and a gray mustache. We talked a little. I felt comfortable with him; he seemed to understand my condition, not judge it.

After the exam was over, the doctor said I was healthy, the baby was growing as it should, and that he would be back in to talk to me after he had seen my blood test.

"Get dressed," he said. "I'll be back in a few minutes."

He came back a few minutes later and said I was anemic. "You'll need to take these pills every day, and I want to see you in two weeks to test your blood again."

He sat down on his little round stool and took a round calendar-type thing from his front pocket.

"When was your last period?" he asked.

"If you want to know the day I conceived, it was August 15th."

"Are you sure about that?" he asked.

"Positive," I said.

"Well, let's see." He started turning the little wheel around and said, "Your due date should be May 8th." I already knew that, but this was my first visit with him and he was making his own records.

AFTER the exam, I went to the waiting room. Miss Miller put down the magazine she had been reading and went to the coat rack and handed me my coat. "Let's go, Becki, it's almost noon and Mrs. Marting wanted you to get started with school after lunch."

After lunch, I went to Mrs. Marting's office. We talked about my school back home and what I had been studying. She had phoned my other school for my records and said they should arrive within the week. I had left so suddenly that all my records hadn't been prepared upon my leaving.

THEN we went to the classroom. Mrs. Riley was our teacher. She was an easy teacher to learn from. She treated us more like friends than students. The first day in school went fine, but I had homework to do that evening.

After supper and after our homework was done we'd all gather down in the card room. I didn't feel much like playing cards that night, so I just watched.

Sandy, who played cards almost every night, had a card game she played by herself. I asked her what she was playing, and she said, "Solitaire," and asked me if I wanted to learn it. I told her I'd just watch and she could show me tomorrow night. What I wanted to learn was how to shuffle the cards the way she did. I watched her and was amazed how she could shuffle those cards so fast and not lose them all over the room. I picked up a deck of cards and started practicing. It took me about a week to get pretty good at shuffling the cards myself. I learned how to play Solitaire and I liked it.

When I had been at the home a little over two weeks I had pretty much settled into the routine of everything.

One Saturday afternoon I was in the bedroom sitting on my bed writing a letter to Greg. Greg had come back from California at the end of October, and when he came over to my house to see me for the first time I tried to pretend everything was the same as it had been before he left. I spent days thinking and rehearsing before I was ready to tell Greg I was pregnant. He sat on our couch for the longest time without saying a word. I couldn't take the silence, and I started crying. Greg was crying too. He wrapped his arms around me and waited until I stopped crying. My head was lying on his chest and his heart was pounding so fast it scared me. He took his arms from around me and stood up looking very pale. I stood up and wrapped my arms around his middle. All I could say was, "I'm sorry, I'm sorry." He took my arms and slowly took them from his waist. He stepped back and took my hand. He patted it and said, "I can't talk to you anymore. I'll call you later." He slowly walked out the door, closing it quietly behind him.

Three days passed and Greg called. He came over and he told me he still loved me and he didn't want us to break up. He told me it was going to take time for him to sort out everything in his mind. I knew things might never be the same between us again and I didn't really expect it to be, but our relationship continued and he had been writing to me at the home almost every night.

As I was writing my letter to Greg, Penny and a new girl walked into the room. Penny introduced me to Amy. Amy was tall and skinny. She had long, dark hair and dark brown eyes. She looked younger than I. Amy said hi to me in a gruff voice, and asked Penny where she was to put her things. Penny pulled out the two bottom drawers of my dresser and told her to put them in there.

Amy was one angry girl. She threw her clothes into the drawers as she sat on the floor. Penny looked at me and shrugged her shoulders and left the room.

Then Amy started crying. "Why did I have to come here, why couldn't I have stayed at home? I'm not even showing yet."

I just couldn't help it. I got off my bed and sat on the floor next to her and put my arms around her. She put her head on my shoulder and cried and cried. When she had finished she lifted her head and wiped her tears away with her hands.

"How old are you?" I asked her.

"Fifteen," she said, "but I'll be sixteen next month. How old are you?"

"Seventeen," I said.

"Are your mom and dad going to let you keep the baby?" Amy asked me.

I said I didn't know. Amy said her mom and dad wouldn't ever let her bring the baby home. She was too young to be a mother and her folks weren't going to help her in any way if she kept the baby. Sounds familiar, I thought to myself. I looked at Amy and she looked at me. Her face was tear-stained and her mascara was all over her face. I couldn't help but laugh. She started laughing too and asked me, "What?" I got up and told her to follow me. We went into the bathroom and I told her to look in the mirror. She started laughing again. I got a wash cloth from the closet and gave it to her.

After she cleaned her face, we went back into the room. I sat down on the floor and took her clothes out of the drawers and started folding them neatly and putting them back in. Then I got up and sat on the bed next to her. She had a hundred questions to ask me. We talked for nearly an hour, and when I looked at the clock it was just about suppertime. "Come on," I said. "Time to eat." Amy followed me to the mess hall, where I introduced her to the rest of the group.

After supper, we went to the card room. Amy sat down next to Sandy and asked her for a cigarette. Sandy frowned at Amy, but gave her one of her cigarettes. I had to tell Amy after we left that if she smoked, she'd better get her own. Bumming cigarettes didn't go over very well at the home. We gave our money to Miss Miller, and she would pick up the cigarettes at the store for us.

Amy and I went to our bathroom and washed our faces and brushed our teeth. After we got our nightgowns on I went and sat on Amy's bed. She looked tired, and much too young to have such dark circles under her eyes. We talked for half an hour before it was time to turn out the lights. I was almost asleep when I heard someone crying. I raised my head and looked around the room. Amy had her covers up over her head and was sobbing quietly. I waited until she stopped crying, and then I went to sleep.

The next morning Amy and I went to breakfast together. After we ate I took her to the classroom. Mrs. Riley introduced herself to Amy and asked her a few questions. Amy was snappy and a little rude to Mrs. Riley, and she didn't pay much attention to anything Mrs. Riley was teaching that day. After school was over for the day Amy and I started up the stairs to our room.

"Amy," I said, "Mrs. Riley is really nice. Why did you talk to her the way you did today?"

Amy glared at me and snapped, "I didn't ask to come to this hell-hole and I'll be damned if I care if anybody here likes me or not."

With that, she ran up the stairs and slammed the bedroom door. I thought I'd just leave Amy alone for a while until she cooled off, so I turned back down the stairs and went to the card room.

Penny was sitting on the couch rubbing her tummy and breathing hard. "What's wrong, Penny?" I asked.

"I think I'm having a contraction," Penny said.

I sat down beside her and asked her if it hurt. "Not really," she said, "this is the fourth one I've had in the last hour." Penny was eight days overdue and we all knew she would be the next one to have her baby. She stood up from the couch and said she had to go to the bathroom. I went to the card table and started shuffling the cards.

About ten minutes had passed and Penny didn't come back. I went to the bathroom and Penny was sitting in one of the stalls. I knocked on the door. "Penny, are you all right?"

"I think my water broke, Becki. Will you go get Mrs. Marting?"

I rushed out of the bathroom and didn't even stop to knock on Mrs. Marting's door, but burst into her office. She was on the phone.

"Mrs. Marting, come quick, Penny needs you. I think her water broke." She told whomever she was talking to she would call back and hung up the phone.

"Calm down, Becki," she said. "Now, where is Peggy?"

"In the bathroom. Come on." I tugged on her arm. She smiled at me and followed.

Mrs. Marting and I brought Penny out of the bathroom and took her to Mrs. Marting's office. Mrs. Marting called the doctor's office and was told to take Penny to the hospital. Mrs. Marting asked Penny what she wanted to take to the hospital, and handed me a brown bag with handles on it and asked me to go to Penny's room to get her things. When I brought Penny's belongings back down to Mrs. Marting's office Miss Miller was there too. Miss Miller took Penny's arm and started out the door.

" 'Bye, Penny," I said.

" 'Bye, Becki." Penny turned and looked at me, a worried and scared look on her face.

I left Mrs. Marting's office and went back down to the card room. Sandy was there and so was Jody. Jody was seventeen years old, a junior in high school. Jody had been at the home the longest of all the girls.

I sat on the couch and said, "Miss Miller just took Penny to the hospital. She's in labor."

Sandy put down her cards and Jody put her knitting in her lap. "I wonder if she'll get to keep her baby," Sandy said.

Jody looked down at her tummy and said, "I don't think so; her folks have told her she's too young to care for a baby and she has to graduate from high school, and then they want her to go on to college. Her folks said they won't support her and the baby. So Penny would have to get a job and her mom won't help her with the baby because she has a good job and she's not going to give up her job to stay home and take care of Penny's baby. Besides that, they hate Penny's boyfriend and they would do anything to break them up."

Jody picked up her knitting and said, "My mom said she would help me if I keep the baby. My baby isn't going home with anybody but me. I'm glad my mom's not like Penny's mom."

I started thinking about my own mom then. Why did she want me here? Was all this to make it easier on her? Where was she? Tears were welling in my eyes now.

"Becki," Jody said, "what about your baby?"

"I don't know," I said. "I was sent here to have the baby and to give her up for adoption. My mother said I have to do what is best for the baby and having a baby without a marriage or a father just isn't right."

"Right for who?" Jody said. "Your mom isn't willing to help because it will disrupt *her* own life. Same old story."

Amy walked into the card room. "Could I talk to you for a minute, Becki?" I walked over to Amy and she said, "Come on." We walked into the hall and she said, "I'm sorry I acted that way with you, it's just so hard being here; maybe things will get better after I've been here for awhile." I assured her it would, and then I told her about Penny.

After supper, when my homework was done, I went upstairs to our bedroom. I didn't feel like playing cards tonight. I crawled into bed and all I could think about was Penny.

I WOKE up at six the next morning. I put on my robe and went to the card room. I lit a cigarette and closed my eyes tight and imagined being home. I would be getting ready for school, Kellee would be over to pick me up soon, and Greg would come over to see me after he got off work. I was imagining my life before I got pregnant. *I* got pregnant! My eyes opened quickly. Mike flashed through my mind. This was the first time I had even thought about him since I had been here. I wondered what he had been doing. Was he in Vietnam? Was he alive? Was he hurt? Was he dead? He doesn't care, why should I? I brushed him out of my mind.

Lights went on in the kitchen. I heard pots and pans rattling and Mrs. Tibbs singing "Your Cheatin' Heart." I went to the kitchen.

"Good morning, Mrs. Tibbs." I had startled her a little.

"Well, Becki, what are you doing down here so early?"

"I just woke up, so I came down to the card room and was just waiting for everyone else to get up."

"Wanna cup of coffee?" she asked.

"Sure, that sounds good."

"It'll be ready in a minute."

"Mrs. Tibbs . . . " I said. She turned to look at me because I didn't continue with my conversation after I said her name.

"What is it, Becki?" She looked at me like a mother would who was concerned about a child who had just been hurt.

"Penny's in the hospital," I said.

"Oh!" Mrs. Tibbs said, with a change of expression on her face. "Is that what it is? I thought something was wrong with you. You know, Becki," she continued, "I've been here for five years now, and I've seen all types of girls coming and going. Some I get close to and some I don't. My job is to feed you well and to make sure those babies are getting the right kind of food. When I first started here, I used to go home and worry about the girls. I knew I was feeding

28

them well, they were getting their schooling, and the doctor was making sure they were healthy and the babies were healthy. But when I'd come in in the mornings and one of the girls wasn't at the breakfast table, I knew she must be having her baby. Most of the girls who are sent here give their babies up for adoption. I'm not saying anything bad about adoption. There are a lot of folks out there wanting a baby of their own and can't have them themselves, and I know they must check out these people awful good before they place a baby with them. So the baby has a good home to go to and the young girls have their own lives to go on with. I just can't help but wonder sometimes." She stopped talking.

"Wonder what?" I thought as I looked at her.

"I gotta stop talking now, Becki, I've got to get breakfast started."

I went upstairs to take my shower. I stood in the shower and looked down at my tummy. It had grown quite a lot since I'd been here. A little ripple went through my tummy. I looked down and could see the movement of my baby. I hugged my tummy. I love you and I'll never let anything happen to you. The baby moved again. She understands, I thought to myself—I had always thought of my baby as a "her." When I talked about the baby, it was "she" or "her."

I put my towel around myself and was brushing my teeth when Amy came in. "I was wondering where you were," she said. "Wanna go hustle up some men tonight, maybe go to a movie or dancing, or something like that?" We both started laughing.

"What's so funny, girls?" Mrs. Marting was just coming up the stairs.

"Oh, nothing," Amy said and pulled a funny face at me.

"How's Penny?" I asked Mrs. Marting.

"I just called the hospital and she's dilated to nine. She should be having the baby soon."

Penny was going to have her baby soon, she wasn't going to have to come back here, she was going to get to go home soon. All I could think about was how lucky Penny was.

After school was over Amy and I went to the card room. We had been there only a few minutes when Sandy came waddling in out of breath.

She was so big I wondered how she could even breathe at all.

"Penny had her baby," she wheezed.

"Are she and the baby all right?" I asked.

"Yeah," Sandy began. "Mrs. Marting said she had a little trouble toward the end. She wanted to quit pushing so the doctor had to use forceps to get the baby the rest of the way out."

"Well, what did she have?" I asked, all excited.

"A little girl," Sandy said.

"Did she see the baby?"

"I don't know," Sandy said, "Mrs. Marting just told me that she'd had the baby."

I told Amy I would be back in a minute and went straight to Mrs. Marting's office. I had to know more about Penny.

"Yes, Becki, what is it?" Mrs. Marting asked as I went into her office.

"Sandy just told us Penny had her baby."

"Yes, she did," Mrs. Marting said.

"Did she see the baby? Did she get to hold her?" I asked.

"No, Becki, they took the baby right out of the room after she was born. Penny's mother didn't want her to see the baby; she thought it would be too hard on Penny if she saw the baby."

I stood there and stared at her.

"Becki, that's why you girls are here. Your parents don't feel you are ready to be mothers and there are a lot of women who can't have their own children. We are here to help both parties involved. You see, Becki, if you don't see your baby, then you won't miss what you don't see."

I could feel myself getting all hot inside. At that moment I didn't even want to be in the same room with Mrs. Marting. I left her office without saying a word and went to my room and lay on my bed.

I must have dozed off. Then Amy came into the room and told me supper was ready. "I've been up a couple of times but you were sleeping so soundly, I thought I'd just let you sleep," she said. "Come on, let's go eat, we get chocolate cake for dessert tonight."

"I'm not hungry, Amy, you go without me."

Amy sat down on my bed. "What's the matter with you, Becki? You act like you're pregnant or something," she said with a chuckle.

"I am pregnant, Amy, and I don't want to have my baby taken away from me like Penny's was."

"So that's what it is," Amy said, her happy face turned sullen.

"Becki, why do you think we're here? We're here to have the babies and to give them up for adoption. A few of the girls get to keep their babies, but I don't think very many do."

"Well, I don't want to be here anymore, Amy, and I'm going to call my mom tonight and tell her I want to come home."

"You're not going to leave here and you know it, Becki. Now let's go eat. You might not be hungry, but you're not just eating for yourself, you know." She patted my stomach and got off the bed and started walking to the door. I got up and followed her.

About a week had passed and it was around ten-thirty in the morning. School was in progress and I needed to go upstairs to Mrs. Marting's office to get some more Kleenex. Several of the girls had colds, and we had used all the Kleenex in the class room. I was in the main entryway and glanced out the window and saw a man standing by the driver's side of a car looking at our building. I heard the main door open, and I peeked around the corner to see who was coming in. Nobody was coming in; it was Penny and her mother going out. Penny's mom was carrying two small suitcases and Penny was holding a small paper bag.

"Penny," I shouted, my voice echoing down the hall. "Are you leaving without saying goodbye to anyone?"

Penny slowly raised her head up to look at me. Penny looked and talked like a little old lady. "Yes, Becki, I'm leaving without telling anyone goodbye. I want to forget this place and everyone in it."

Penny's mom gave me a faint smile and started walking down the steps to the car. "Hurry up, Penny, your dad has to get back to work," she said looking straight ahead. Penny's shoulders were slumped.

"Are you all right?" I asked.

"I'm still just a little sore, Becki, but I'll be fine." Penny's lip started quivering and she burst out in tears. "They took my baby, all I know is that she was a baby girl. I had to sign the adoption papers yesterday, and I hate my parents so much, I'll never forgive them, never."

Penny's dad was still standing outside by the car door. He yelled at Penny, "Come on, Penny, right now! I have to get back to work!" And with that he got in the car and slammed the door.

"I gotta go now, Becki," Penny said, wiping her nose with her coat sleeve. She opened up her arms and I put my arms around her. "Goodbye, Becki."

"Goodbye, Penny."

She walked slowly down the steps and got into the back seat of the car. She looked straight ahead as the car drove off.

I was shivering when I went back inside. It was snowing lightly and I brushed the snowflakes off my clothes and went upstairs to my bedroom. I crawled into bed and pulled the covers up around me. I was so cold I couldn't stop shivering. I knew Mrs. Riley would send someone to find me when I didn't return to the classroom, so I lay in bed and waited.

About ten minutes later Amy came in the room. "What's the matter, Becki?"

"I guess it's just this cold I have. I'm not feeling very well today," I said. "Amy, will you tell Mrs. Riley I'm not feeling very good and will you bring me my homework for today when school's out?"

"Sure," Amy said, "see ya later."

Now I knew I would be left alone for a while. I had to think. After seeing Penny today and seeing how brokenhearted she was, I knew more than ever I had to leave this place. I had to get home, and I had to keep my baby. I would call Mom tonight and tell her about Penny, tell her I didn't want to be here, ask her for the hundredth time why I had to be here. This was *my* baby and nobody was going to do to me what they had done to Penny.

I didn't go to lunch, and by suppertime I was hungry. I went to the mess hall and sat down by Amy.

"Feeling any better?" Amy asked.

"A little," I said. I told Amy about calling my mom tonight and telling her I wanted to come home. Amy looked at me like I was an idiot.

"She's not gonna let you come home. You're just wasting your time," Amy said in a matter-of-fact voice.

"We'll see about that," I said. I picked up my plate and glass and slammed them down on the kitchen counter. I went to the pay phone in the hall and closed the door behind me. I dialed my home number and Mom answered. I told her about Penny, how homesick I was, how unhappy I was, and I begged her to come and get me and take me home.

"No, Rebecca, I'm not coming to get you, you're staying there until the baby comes. How are you doing in school?" she changed the subject.

"Fine," I said. "I have to go now, Mom. I'll call you Sunday."

"Rebecca, I love you."

"I love you too, Mom. Goodbye."

Click.

Amy was waiting for me in the hall. "What did she say, is she gonna come get you?"

"No," I said.

"I told you she wouldn't, didn't I?" Amy started crying. "I don't want you to leave, Becki. I don't want to be here by myself. Please don't leave, Becki."

I put my arm over Amy's shoulder and tugged on her hair. "Come on," I said, "let's go play cards."

It was now almost the middle of February and my eighteenth birthday was just a few days off. I had often thought about what I was going to do on my eighteenth birthday. Have my friends over, drink some beer, eat pizza, and stay out all night partying. So much for that thought.

My birthday came and the best I could expect was the little cake Mrs. Tibbs would bake. After school was over I stopped at Mrs. Marting's office to see if I had any mail. She handed me a whole handful of letters. I thought they must be all birthday cards because they weren't in the usual letter envelopes.

"Happy birthday, Becki," Mrs. Marting said.

"Thanks," I said.

I got to my room and there on my table were eighteen beautiful red roses! I opened the card that came with them and it was from my dad! I still missed my dad very much.

That's it, I thought, Dad will help me! He'll come get me. But then I saw my mother's face and remembered her words: "Your father left us to be with that other woman. He doesn't care about us. He walked out of our lives; he threw us all out like an old shoe. If he had loved you kids he wouldn't have left us." So much for that thought, I told myself.

I opened up all my birthday cards. One from Greg, Kellee, Pat, Carla, Tracy, my brother and my two sisters and one from Mom. Mom had sent me some money so I could buy myself something next time we went to the little shopping mall near the home. The roses, the cards and to top it off, when I got my cake that night, the girls sang, "Happy Birthday!" It wasn't the birthday I had planned for so long, but it was a nice birthday just the same.

Several days passed and Sandy went into labor. Sandy was a tough girl. She talked tough, acted like she couldn't care less about anybody or anything. She was always cussing about something. When she talked about her baby it was always "the kid." Sandy was my age, but she looked a lot older. I had given Sandy money before so she could buy cigarettes. Her family didn't have very much to give her, so I didn't mind giving it to her when she needed it.

Sandy had a baby girl. She weighed almost nine pounds. Sandy got to see her baby. She told the social worker she wasn't going to sign any damn papers if they wouldn't let her see her baby. She got to hold her baby and feed her and then she told her goodbye.

A few days later Sandy came to pack up her things. A few of us girls followed her to her old bedroom. She started shoving her clothes into her old, torn suitcase.

"What about your baby, Sandy?" I asked her.

"I'm giving her up for adoption. I'll be damned if my kid's gonna grow up like I did. No father, never enough money, Mom working all day and boozing all night long. My kid's gonna have better than me." She slammed her suitcase lid. "Fuck this place, I'm outta here! 'Bye guys." Now Sandy was gone.

Being cooped up in this place was really starting to wear on all of us. Mrs. Marting didn't want us going out for walks because she

34

was afraid someone would slip on the ice and hurt herself or her baby.

Some of us would put on our coats and just sit on the front steps of the home. We would watch the cars go by and every once in a while someone would walk by. No one would even look our way.

It was the first week in March and the sun was shining and the snow had melted off the sidewalks. It was Saturday and Amy and I decided we would walk to the little shopping center just to get out of the building. When we left we had to sign out on the list by the back door, and we had to sign in again when we got back.

It was still a little bit chilly outside, but the sun felt good on our faces. We were a couple of blocks from the shopping center when a car drove by with four boys in it.

They stopped and started backing up. "Hey, girls, wanna ride?" one yelled. Amy and I must have been thinking the same thing, because at the same time we both opened up our coats and showed our swollen bellies, and yelled, "Sure." The boy hanging out the window dropped his mouth open and slid back in the seat and motioned to his friend to get going. Amy and I started laughing so hard and all Amy could say was, "I'm gonna wet my pants."

"So much for hustling guys," I said.

We got to the shopping center and just walked around looking in the windows. We went inside one of the department stores. It was pretty warm inside, so we took our coats off. People started looking at us as if we both had horrible disfigurements. I had never before been looked at as though I were something distasteful.

My feelings were hurt, and Amy was just plain mad. I had just learned why I had been put in that home: we were to be hidden from the view of nice, respectable people like those at the shopping centers.

"What are you looking at, you old cow?" Amy hissed. I didn't even look at who she had said that to. I tugged on her arm, "Let's go, Amy." Amy cursed and stomped all the way back to the home, and all I could think about were those faces looking at me the way they did.

After we got back to the home and checked in we went to the card room. Mary, one of the newest girls who had been put in our bedroom, said, "About ten minutes after you two left, Jody started having some real hard contractions. She's already left for the hospital."

My thoughts were of Jody. Her time here was over, her baby not inside her anymore. She would finish school and go on to who knows what. Jody's baby came fast. She wasn't in labor fifteen or twenty hours like some of the other girls. Jody had a son. Jody had her son on a Saturday and on the following Wednesday Jody came back to the home.

Jody was not alone. She held in her arms her newborn son, Tyler J. All the girls gathered around Jody and Tyler. "He's beautiful!" "Look at those tiny hands!" "Oh look, he's opening up his eyes!" Everyone was talking and admiring Jody's son.

"Oh, Jody," I said, "I'm so happy for you! You meant every word you said to me about keeping your baby."

"Yes, Becki, I meant every word of it. It may be hard for awhile, but we'll do just fine. My mom is going to help me, and she just loves him so much." Jody hugged Tyler close to her and kissed him on the forehead.

"Girls!" A sharp, shrill voice yelled out. We all turned. It was Mrs. Marting. "You all have things to do around here; let's let Jody get upstairs and get her things packed." With that, she pivoted on her heels and walked into her office and shut the door. We all turned and looked at Jody.

Jody's face hardened, and she spoke in a firm and controlled voice. "Mrs. Marting thought all along my talk of keeping my baby was just wishful thinking. She sent some social worker to the hospital to try to talk some sense into my head. This lady didn't know my mom was standing outside the door listening to everything she was saying to me until she got to 'How unfair and unfortunate for this child to be raised a bastard. A young girl not even out of high school, no job, no way of knowing what's involved in raising a child.'

"Then Mom came into the room. She told this social worker to call Mrs. Marting and tell her the plan hadn't worked.

" 'My daughter is keeping her baby, and now, if you will, please leave.' The social worker just gathered up some papers and stomped out of the room.

"Mrs. Marting is mad at me because I'm keeping Tyler. That doesn't happen very often around here, as you well know. I could care less what she thinks or anybody else.

"Well," Jody said, "I had better get my things. Mom's waiting for me in the car and we have to stop at the store and get some things for the baby."

Amy and I went upstairs and helped Jody bring her suitcases down. Jody's mom was standing just inside the main door now. We handed her the suitcases and I opened the door for her.

"Goodbye, girls," she said in a soft, concerned voice. Jody gave us all a hug and I kissed Tyler on the cheek. Then they were gone.

"What do you want to do, Becki?" Amy said, after Jody had left. "You wanna play some cards or something?"

"Why don't you go to the card room, Amy. I'll be down in a little bit," I said.

"Okay." Amy turned toward the basement. I went upstairs and lay on my bed and turned on the little radio on my night stand.

The song coming out of the radio was "Lonely Girl." I had heard that song before, but this time I really listened to it. When it was over I burst into a fit of sobs, holding my breath, gasping, sobbing. I had just lost my mind. I was no longer in control of myself. I rolled over on my stomach, gathering my knees up beneath me so as not to hurt the baby, and lay my face in my open hands. All of a sudden a feeling came over me. I felt like a mother bear who was watching as something was about to harm her cubs. I felt I needed to protect someone from some horrible event about to happen. I had never had such a strong sense of urgency in my life. I bolted up out of my crouched position and sat upright on my bed. I have to get home, I thought. I have to get home.

That evening I phoned my mom again. This time I cried. I hadn't cried before when I pleaded for her to come get me and take me home, but this time I did. Same old answers from her.

I called Kellee next, and her mother answered the phone. "Will you accept a collect call from Becki?" the operator asked and we waited a few seconds before Kellee's mom spoke. Kellee's mom was a very nice lady, but very strict. I don't think she ever liked me because whenever Kellee got into trouble or was home late I always seemed to be in the picture. I think she always thought everything was my fault. Now, after her short silence, Kellee's mom said "Yes, just a minute and I'll get her." Then Kellee came on the phone.

"Kellee, listen," I said. "I have to come home. I can't stay here any longer. Please, please, go over to my house tomorrow and talk to my mom. She won't listen to me. I need some help, will you do that for me?"

"Becki, you know I will," she said, "what's the matter?"

I told her I would write a letter tonight and explain why I had to leave. "Kellee, I'm going to call you collect tomorrow night and see what my mom says. Please tell your mom I'll send the money for the phone calls. I miss you Kel, 'bye."

I called Kellee the next night and learned that my mom had told her the very same thing she had been telling me: I was staying at the home no matter what, until "it" was all over, then I could come home.

I was calling Mom every other night now pleading with her, but to no avail. It was now the last week in March and my baby was due in about six weeks. Then one night Mom refused to accept my collect call.

THE next morning I was called in to Mrs. Marting's office.

"Becki, come and sit down. I need to talk to you," she said. "Your mother has phoned me on several occasions telling me that you are phoning her almost every night for her to come get you. Becki, you are doing so well in school, all A's in every class; you get along well with the other girls, and I haven't been told of any problems that you are having. So exactly what is going on?"

I kept my head lowered and felt my lower lip quivering. I wasn't going to start crying in front of her, so I bit my upper lip until my eyes quit watering. "I don't want to have my baby here. I want my mother to be with me." That was all I could say.

"Becki," Mrs. Marting began, "I can understand your wanting your mother to be with you; but this is what your mother wanted for you. She wants you to finish your stay here and go home after the baby is born."

"And I'm not to take the baby home either, am I?" I was getting angry now. "So what about my baby? Do I just hand her over to you and go home and pretend none of this happened?"

"Yes, Becki, that's exactly what you'll do. You will go home and go back to school and graduate and go on to college or whatever you want to do, and you *will* forget about the baby. You will be married someday and have more babies of your own, but your children will also have a father. This is why we have adoption. You girls can solve your problems and give your child to a loving couple who have tried but couldn't have their own baby. We screen these couples very closely, and you can be sure your baby will be placed in a very good home."

I didn't want to hear any more, I just wanted to get out of there.

"We'll talk again, Becki, if you need to. You don't have that much longer to be here; you'll be going home soon enough. Okay?"

"Okay," I said, and left her office.

It was now the first week in April. I had a little over a month before my due date. The last two weeks I hadn't slept very well. I would lie awake and think of something different to tell my mom—something, anything. I *was* going home, and that was all there was to it.

On April the 3rd, I was too tired to argue with Mom on the phone anymore, so when I called her I told her I was coming home. I had twenty-four dollars, which wasn't enough for a bus ticket, but I was leaving in the morning anyway. I was going to hitchhike home. I was going to take only my small suitcase and I would send for the rest of my things once I got home.

"Mom," I continued, "if I get hit by a car or if I'm picked up and murdered or whatever can happen to someone hitchhiking, then that's the way this is all going to end. I'm tired; I'm so tired. I can't and I won't argue with you anymore, but I'm coming home. Goodbye, Mom."

I went upstairs and took out my small red suitcase and sat it on the bed. Amy was sitting on her bed writing a letter.

"What do you think you're doing, Becki? Why do you have your suitcase out?"

39

"I'm leaving in the morning, Amy," I said.

"Becki, please don't go! You can't go! I'm not staying here without you."

We were both crying now. "Amy, listen to me. When I began to tell you I had to go home, I wasn't just saying that to hear myself talk. I can't explain what it is; it has me a little scared, but I have to leave *now*. I don't know what it is, Amy, honest I don't, but I can't have my baby here."

For the first time since I began telling Amy that I was leaving, she seemed to have a look of understanding in her eyes. "I'm going to miss you, Becki. It's not going to be the same here without you."

"I'm going to miss you too, Amy." We gave each other a hug.

Then Mary walked into our room. "Becki, Mrs. Marting sent me up here to get you. She wants to talk to you. What's your suitcase out for?" she asked.

"I'm leaving," I said as I walked out of the room. I could hear Amy and Mary talking as I went down the stairs.

I walked into Mrs. Marting's office and found her standing by her desk, her hands pressed tightly on its top. "I just got a phone call from your mother," she said. I just looked at her and waited to hear the same old thing. "She is leaving tonight with a friend and they are driving here and should be in tomorrow afternoon some time. She's coming to take you home. She also wanted me to make it perfectly clear that you will go to the Morris's home in Boise and continue your schooling and continue with everything just the same as if you were here. I have also told your mother that I don't agree with her decision to come and get you. I have no idea what you could possibly have said to her to change her mind, but I just want you to know I think you are making a big mistake. I'll see you tomorrow when I sign your discharge slip. Goodnight."

"Goodnight, Mrs. Marting," I said.

I stopped at the bottom of the stairs. I took a deep breath and held on to the banister. No more stairs, I thought to myself.

THE next morning I went to class as usual and told Mrs. Riley I would be leaving today. She looked surprised. She asked me a few questions.

"I believe you know what you are doing, Becki; I just hope someday you will be happy again."

I asked Mrs. Riley for my grades and the papers I would need to start school at the other Morris home. Mrs. Riley said she would get everything in order and take it up to Mrs. Marting's office. She was so understanding and I knew I was going to miss her. She put her arms around me and I hugged her back.

"I'm going to miss you, Becki," she said.

"I'm going to miss you too, Mrs. Riley." I really meant it.

Mom and her friend Vera arrived at the home around three-thirty that afternoon. They both looked awfully tired. I asked Mom if they had slept anywhere and she said they had a little bit. I told Mom I had everything ready and that I would go upstairs and get my things and I would be right down.

Amy was sitting on my bed when I got upstairs. We had become good friends and I was going to miss her very much.

"Amy, my mom is here. I'm leaving now."

"Becki, promise me you'll write to me and call me sometime, okay?"

"You know I will, Amy."

Amy walked downstairs with me. Mom and Mrs. Marting were talking as we walked into the hallway.

"Becki," said Mrs. Marting, "I need you to sign your name on this discharge form before you leave." Those words sounded so good to me.

The girls came to tell me goodbye and they all gave me a hug. "I'll walk to the car with you," Amy said. I told Mrs. Marting goodbye. Vera took my suitcases and put them in the trunk. Mom and Vera got in the car. Neither Amy nor I wanted to cry when we said goodbye, but we just couldn't help it. I felt I had betrayed Amy in some way, but we were going to have to say goodbye sooner or later anyway, and I was glad it was sooner. I got in the back seat and the car started. We were really leaving. I turned to look at Amy; she just stood there and stared at the car.

WE drove for several hours, but Mom and Vera were tired so we stopped at a motel to spend the night. We got up early the next morning and continued on our way. Around two in the afternoon, Vera was wanting a piece of pie and a cup of coffee, so we stopped in a little town and went into a truck stop. I had been cramped in the back seat and all I wanted to do was to walk around and stretch my legs. I was getting the same looks from the people in the cafe that I had gotten from the people at the shopping center. I went to the table and sat down and pulled my chair as close to the table as I could. I just wanted to scream at all of them, "I'm just pregnant! I promise you won't catch it." Mom was embarrassed, but Vera knew I was feeling self-conscious and she smiled at me, "Let's go, the pie was awful anyway."

We were close to home now, and I could feel myself getting excited.

"We will be home in a few minutes," Mom said. Home. That's good, I thought, I need to be home.

We drove up into the driveway. The house looked good. I couldn't wait to get inside. The first room I wanted to see or be in was my own room. The door was open and I walked in. Everything was the same as I'd left it. Good, I thought. I opened up my closet door. My clothes were all there; jeans, sweatshirts, miniskirts, tight shirts. I couldn't wait to get back into my old clothes; I was so tired of maternity clothes.

We had only been home for about ten minutes when the doorbell rang. "Rebecca, would you get that?" Mom called out from the kitchen. I opened the front door and there stood Kellee, Carla and Pat. My mouth fell open.

"Hi, Becki," they all said. "We've been waiting over at Kellee's most of the day. Your mom said she would call us as soon as you guys got into town, and here we are!" I hugged them all.

"Gosh, Becki," Kellee said, "you're big!"

"Yeah, I know, and I've still got another month to go."

They all took turns patting my tummy. The baby started moving. "Look guys," I said and pulled up my shirt and pulled my pants down a little. The baby must have been trying to find a more comfortable position, and the punching and poking she was doing inside just fascinated my friends. They just stood there and stared and giggled.

This was all new to them of course, but I had grown used to it. The baby's dropped an awful lot, I thought to myself as I held my shirt up watching the movement inside of me.

"Becki, do you feel like going to the park with us?" Kellee asked. Mom was standing in the living room now; I looked at her and she nodded her head. "Go ahead if you feel like it, but I want you home in a couple of hours. It's been a long day and you need to get some rest."

It felt so good to be with my friends again. We drove through the park, and there, sitting on one of the picnic tables, was Greg. "Kellee, Kellee!" Greg yelled as he jumped off the picnic table and ran over to the car. He reached the car and looked inside. I was sitting in the back and he didn't look in the back for a few minutes. Finally he looked in the back. "Becki!" I started laughing as he stood there staring at me. "When did you get home? I didn't even know you were coming. Can I take you home, can we talk?"

I told Kellee and the girls I'd call them tomorrow and got out of the car and went with Greg. We got into Greg's car. He sat there and stared at me. I was feeling very self-conscious. Greg hadn't seen me all swollen and out of proportion like this before. I must be disgusting to him, I thought: I was sitting in the car with him, with another man's baby inside of me; he must be ashamed of me.

Greg laid his head on the steering wheel and started to cry. "Why, Becki, why? Why isn't that my baby?" "I'm sorry, Greg," was all I could get out of me. "You're so beautiful, Becki, do you know that?"

"Beautiful, Greg? I thought I must be disgusting to you."

"Never, Becki." Greg put his hand on my stomach. "How's the little guy doing anyway?" he asked.

"She's fine, Greg. Greg, I'm tired, could you take me home?"

I curled up in my bed and lay my head down on my foam rubber pillow. I closed my eyes and drifted off to sleep.

At four in the morning I awoke with a start. My bed was all wet. So was I. I got out of bed and turned the light on. I threw back the covers and saw a round ring of wetness on the sheets.

My God, I thought, what's the matter? Oh God, my water broke. It's too soon. I have another month. The baby! Something is wrong with the baby! The car ride, it was too bumpy. The stress, not enough sleep, I forgot my vitamins. My head was spinning. What had I done wrong? Is this why I had to come home when I did, did I know the baby was coming early, could I have possibly known that? No! I must have done something wrong, I just knew it. I sat back on the bed and cradled my tummy. I'm sorry, please be all right, I'll take care of you.

My wet gown was sticking to me and I was cold. I had to get out of bed and get cleaned up. I went to the bathroom and took off my nightgown. Don't take a bath—if your water breaks, don't take a bath, you may cause an infection. That was what I had learned at the home. What else am I supposed to do? Calm down, Becki, you can take a shower. I took a shower and went to my room and changed the sheets. It was only four-thirty in the morning. I could wait to get Mom up. This wasn't supposed to happen. I had another month to go. I needed that month to convince Mom that I was keeping my baby.

I was trying so hard to convince myself that my water hadn't broken until my first contraction came. My abdomen began doing something that I wasn't controlling. It was tight and hard. I started praying. God, I'll do anything, just let my baby be all right. I laid three towels on top of my bed and lay down on them.

I continued to make promises to God until six o'clock. It was time to get Mother up. I was scared and didn't want to be alone anymore.

"Mom, Mom," I shook her gently. Her eyes flew open and she bolted upright.

"What, what's the matter?"

"My water broke, I was sleeping when it happened."

She threw her covers back and almost fell as she jumped out of bed. She ran to my room and pulled the covers back. "Where, where?" she screamed.

"Mom, settle down," I said. "I changed the sheets; I put them down the laundry chute."

"Rebecca, how do you know your water broke? Was it a lot? You have another month, are you sure?"

"Yes, Mom, I'm sure."

"What time did this happen?"

"At four o'clock."

"Why didn't you wake me up? Are you all right?"

"I'm fine, Mom, just settle down, will you?" She was walking through the house, mumbling to herself, and wringing her hands. Is this what everybody goes through when they're about to have a baby? "Mom, will you sit down for a minute, we need to talk." She didn't want to sit down but she did. "Mom, what do we do now?" I asked.

"I don't know," she said. "Call the hospital. That's it, I'll call the hospital." She ran to the phone; her voice was shaking as she spoke. "Okay, I'll do that, 'bye. Rebecca, she told me to go over to Morris's first and then they will tell us what to do next. I'm going to take a shower; you go put a few things together to take to the hospital."

Driving to Morris's with Mom was a nightmare. Brake, accelerate, brake, accelerate. "Mom, you're making me sick, can I drive?"

"No. Are you having any more contractions?"

"Just having one now." Accelerate!

We got to Morris's and a woman showed us into a room. "A nurse will be with you in a minute; just sit down and she will be in shortly." The nurse came in. Mom told her the baby was coming early, and told her the whole story. "Well, let's take a look, Becki, and see what's going on." She examined me and told us that I was dilated to three. "She's in labor, all right." The nurse filled out some paper and handed it to Mom. "You will need to go to the hospital right now. I'll contact the hospital and tell them you are coming. They will take it from there."

We were back in the car again. "Let's see, which is the fastest way to the hospital?" Mom asked. "Mom, I'm not going to have the baby in the car, settle down, will you?" "I'll settle down when we get there, now hush." It was eight o'clock and the traffic was heavy. Mom swerved in and out of lanes, cutting people off. She even ran a stoplight. I just slid down farther in my seat and didn't say anything else.

We arrived at the hospital and went to the admitting desk. A wheelchair was sitting by the desk. "Sit down in the wheelchair, dear, and a girl will come and take you upstairs while your mother fills out the admission papers," the woman behind the desk said to me. I had barely sat down when a young girl about my age came over and said she was taking me upstairs now. "Mom, come up as soon as you're done, okay?" "I will, Rebecca. I'll be there in a little bit."

I was taken to a room and was told to undress and put on the hospital gown. A nurse came in and took my blood pressure. "How's everything going?" she asked. "I'm okay, just a little scared," I said. "I know. I had my first one a year ago; it's not so bad," she smiled. "Now, this is what we are going to do before the doctor comes to examine you. I'm going to give you an enema and then I'm going to shave you and then you will be ready for the doctor to see you." Shave me! Oh God, how embarrassing!

Everything was done and I was told to get into bed and the doctor would be with me soon. I was alone in the room, yet there were two other beds. Why was I alone? I could hear some faint whimpering and cries outside my room; someone else was in labor too. She was having a hard time of it, I thought. The doctor came in and examined me. "Everything's progressing nicely, Becki," he said. "Let me know when you have your next contraction.

"Becki, your baby is going to be premature," the doctor said. "I know you already knew that, but let me explain a few things to you. Your baby probably won't weigh more than four pounds, if even that. We won't know what to expect until the baby is born. I just want you to know that the baby is going to be small and will have to be put in an incubator. I need you to help me on one thing, though. If you are having a lot of pain, I can give you a mild dose of something to help ease it a little; but I don't want to give you anything that might slow the baby down any. This baby is going to have to be born as close to naturally as possible. Do you understand what I'm telling you?"

"Yes," I said. "What made me go into labor so soon, did I do something wrong?"

"Becki, you didn't do anything 'wrong,' " he said. "I talked to your mother before I came in here. She told me about the last month at the home and how you wanted to come home so badly. It could very well be that stress and the trip home may have contributed to your early labor, but that's really hard to say. Sometimes premature labor just starts on its own with no reason and no one at fault."

The doctor left to make his rounds, and Mom came into the room. "Is everything all right?" she asked.

"Just fine, Mom. The doctor says the baby is going to be awfully small. I'm scared for the baby, Mom."

"It will be just fine, don't you worry."

"Mom? When you were having us kids, did it hurt a lot?"

"I really don't remember much about it. We had twilight sleep. I was put to sleep and when I woke up the baby was born."

"Did your contractions hurt?"

"I don't remember, I was asleep." Well, so much for that conversation.

"Rebecca, I'm going to go home now and unpack my things and do some washing," said Mom. "The nurse said you would be fine, and they have our home phone number if you need me. I'll be back in a few hours. See you in a little bit."

" 'Bye, Mom," I said. "Oh, Mom, will you call Kellee after school and tell her where I am?"

"Okay," she promised. "Goodbye."

I walked around the room and down the hall a few times. That poor woman down the hall was making all sorts of noise now. She was in pain. I went back to the room and got into bed. And fell asleep until another contraction woke me up. They were getting stronger, further apart, but longer. The nurse came in to check on me. I told her I was hungry and asked for something to eat. "I can't give you anything until after you have the baby; sorry. Ring the buzzer if you need me."

I looked at the clock. School's out now, I thought. I hope Mom calls Kellee. Where is Mom anyway, she left hours ago and she said she would be back soon. I'll wait, she'll be here soon. I have to think now. No, I have to pray now.

I had always been good at talking to God when I was in trouble or when I was sad. Talking to God always made me feel better.

My thoughts went back to the night my grandpa died. Mom,

Dad, my brother and sisters and I had been to see Grandpa the day he died. He had cancer and had gone from a large, healthy two hundred and ten-pound man to a ninety-eight-pound, shriveled-up, sickly old man. We all gave Grandpa a kiss goodbye that day, when it was time to leave the hospital. "I love you, Grandpa," I said as I left the room. He raised his hand and gave me a weak wave bye-bye. "I'll see you tomorrow, okay?" That night, before I went to bed, I got down on my knees by my bed. "Please, God," I prayed, "Grandpa has suffered so much, please don't make him suffer anymore, please let Grandpa die tonight so he can be with you. Please don't let him hurt anymore. Thank you, God, good-night."

I was asleep when the doorbell woke me up. I got out of bed and opened my door. Mom was crying. "Oh Joe, he's gone." My dad had just been told by the family doctor that his dad had just died. Grandpa was dead. I crawled back into bed. I looked up at the ceiling. "Thank you, God," I said. I had always felt that my prayer to God that night was why Grandpa died. I had saved Grandpa from suffering anymore. I was twelve years old then, and from that time on I had always felt that God was listening to me.

"Please, God," I prayed now, "help my baby. I'll do anything, I promise. Please just let my baby be all right."

"Hi, Becki!" My eyes opened, and in walked Kellee, Carla, Pat, and Mom. "The girls wanted to see you," Mom said, "so I waited for them to come to the house and they followed me to the hospital. How are you doing?"

"I'm doing fine. The contractions are coming a lot more often and they hurt a little more, but everything is okay."

The girls stayed and talked to me for awhile, then the nurse came in and told them it was time for them to leave. I was glad the nurse asked them to leave. Every contraction I had since they arrived was hard and painful, but I tried to be brave and not show them how much I was hurting.

" 'Bye, guys," I said, "I'll call you tomorrow and tell you what I had."

Kellee came to the bed and took my hand; she had tears in her eyes. "I'm sorry you hurt, Becki. I love you. I'll see you tomorrow." She let go of my hand and walked out of the room.

Mom stayed for a couple of hours watching me hold my stomach, bring my knees up to my chest, and roll over on my side. It was hard for her to see me like that without being able to help me.

Mom started crying, and the nurse came in. She put an arm on Mom's shoulder. "What's the matter, Mrs. Rankin?" she asked.

"It's so hard watching Rebecca go through this, can't you do anything?"

"No," said the nurse. "Becki isn't completely dilated yet. It may be hours before the baby comes. Why don't you go home and get some rest? I'll call you as soon as it looks like the baby is coming."

"Is that all right with you, Rebecca?" Mom took my hand.

"That's okay, Mom, just be back, okay?"

"I will," Mom said, and left.

I looked at the clock on the wall. It was ten-thirty at night. It seemed like I had been here forever.

My next contraction was different; it was the hardest one I had had, and it made me grab the buzzer and ring for the nurse. The nurse came right in. I had my knees up and I was pushing. "Are you feeling like you need to push now, Becki?" "Yes," I moaned. "I'm calling the doctor now, I'll be right back in." I looked at the clock; it was about ten minutes to eleven.

Soon the nurse came back. "I'll be taking you to the delivery room in just a little bit."

"My mom," I said.

"Oh! I forgot. I'll call her now."

Mom raced into the room just as the nurse was about to wheel me into the delivery room. "Mom, you're here." "Yes, I'm here," she said. "It's going to be over soon now."

The nurse took me to the delivery room. "Slide over onto this table," the nurse said. "I'll help you." I lay on the table and looked up at the large bright light over me. My legs were put into the stirrups. "Slide down a little, Becki," the nurse said. She took my hand and put a strap around my wrist.

"What are you doing?" I asked. "Why are you strapping me down?"

"The doctor doesn't want you touching yourself down there or moving your arms around when the baby's being born." She said something else about infection, but I wasn't listening anymore, I was too busy trying to get my arms free.

The doctor came in. "Becki, I need you to help me. The baby's coming now." I forgot about my arms being tied down now, and started pushing. I pushed until I couldn't push anymore. "I'm too tired, I don't want to push anymore, I'm going to go to sleep now," I told the doctor. "No, you're not," the doctor spoke firmly. "One more push, Becki." I pushed with everything I had left in me and the baby was out.

Silence. Everything was so quiet. All I could hear was my own breathing. I raised my head up and looked around the room. I couldn't see my baby. Two nurses were standing in the corner of the room, their backs to me.

"You had a girl," the doctor said.

"She's not crying," I said. "What's wrong? Is she all right? Let me see her."

A faint cry came from over in the corner. "She's fine, Becki," and with that the nurse walked out of the room with my baby. I laid my head back on the table. "She cried, she's all right," I murmured. "What, what did you say, Becki?" The doctor was pressing on my tummy now. "Oh, nothing," I said. "Will you please untie my arms now?" I asked the nurse who was taking my blood pressure. "As soon as the doctor is done and we clean you up, then I'll undo the straps." This nurse was a large woman, no chin, just all neck. She didn't look like a friendly person.

The nurse who had been with me during my labor came back into the room and stood by my side. "Your baby is fine," she said. "She weighs only four pounds thirteen ounces. We've put her in an incubator. She's really pretty, Becki." I started to cry and asked her one question after another. She had her hand on my shoulder. She had been so nice to me, she hadn't made me feel as though I should be ashamed of myself at all.

The large nurse then came over to the other side of me with a syringe in her hand. She pulled up the sleeve of my gown and pushed the needle into my arm. "What's that for?" the "nice" nurse asked. I thought maybe it was for the pain, or something they gave every woman who had just had a baby. "It's the dry-up shot, it's to dry up her milk. She's not keeping the baby." She shot a glance at the other nurse and walked off.

I watched as the large nurse was walking away. "Who told you that!" I yelled at her.

"Your mother did."

She left the room. My nose was running, tears were falling in my ears. Damn these straps. "Will you untie me now?" I asked the nurse. "I want to blow my nose." She looked at the doctor and he nodded yes. "I'm almost done, Becki. I had to make a little cut, and I just had to put in a few stitches. The baby was small enough, but I didn't want you to tear so I made a small cut. There, you're all done now, Becki. I'll see you tomorrow."

"Thank you, Dr. Edwards," I sobbed.

"There, there," he patted my leg, "you'll be just fine."

The nurse wheeled me out of the delivery room. "We're going to your room now, Becki." Mom was waiting in the hall and walked with us to my room. We passed a few rooms and I saw a mother holding her baby and nursing it. We left the wing of the maternity ward. I wasn't staying in a room with the other mothers, or even on the same floor. I had a private room with a bed next to the window. The nurse helped me into bed and said she would be back in a few minutes.

It was just Mom and I in the room now. "Mom," I began, "a nurse in the delivery room gave me a shot to dry up my milk. She told me you said I wasn't keeping the baby. Why did you tell her that?"

"Because you are not keeping the baby. We have already discussed that."

"Mom, why do you think I wanted to come home so badly? I was going to have a month so we could talk and work out how we were going to take care of the baby."

"Rebecca, no more talk tonight, you are tired and I'm tired. I'm going home now. I'll see you in the morning." She kissed my cheek and left. I am tired, I thought, I'll think tomorrow. I only had enough time to thank God for letting my baby be all right, then I went to sleep.

THE SUN SHONE THROUGH the window and warmed my bed coverings. I lay in bed for a moment. My hands went directly to my stomach. It was flat and I could feel the loose skin. I pulled up my gown to look at my tummy. It wasn't swollen and there was no one in there moving around or kicking me any more. I knew I was going to miss rubbing my tummy and talking to that little person inside of me. I felt very lonely all of a sudden, a part of me wasn't there anymore.

I put my legs over the side of the bed. Should I just get up and go to the bathroom or do I have to ring for the nurse? I didn't want to get scolded like I was when I got up at four-thirty. I had awakened and had to go to the bathroom. I didn't know I wasn't supposed to get out of bed. I didn't know I was supposed to ring for a nurse and use a bed pan. Instead, I got out of bed and went to the bathroom and was standing by the bed just about to get back in when a nurse came into the room. She gasped and ran over to grab my arm. "What on earth are you doing out of bed?" she snapped. "I had to go to the bathroom," I said. "Well, then, you just get back into that bed and I'll bring you a bed pan." "But I already went." I gave a little grin. "Oh my God," she said as she drew her breath in. "You could have gotten dizzy and fallen and hurt yourself. Don't you know you are weak after having had a baby? What on earth were you thinking?" "I was just thinking I had to go to the bathroom, that's all," I said. Her face and voice softened a little. "You really didn't have any problems when you got up, you weren't dizzy or anything?" "I just walked real slow, that's all," I said. "Well, okay," she said as she helped me back into bed.

"You ring for me if you need to use the bathroom, all right?" "Okay," I said.

I decided I had better ring for a nurse this time, even though I didn't want to. The nurse came in about five minutes later. "Good morning," she said with a smile and a big, deep dimple on each cheek that sunk into her face as she smiled. "I was looking at your chart before I came in. It looks like you had a pretty good night, huh?"

"Yes," I said, "but the nurse came in quite a few times to take my blood pressure and temperature and to check my pad."

"Well, I know that's a bother, but it's hospital procedure and we have to follow the rules. Heard you got out of bed this morning without any help."

"Yeah," I said, "I got told off, too."

"Oh that Doris, she's a funny one. She's so worried about someone getting hurt on her shift, she's so careful in doing everything 'just right.' She just mothers all of her patients, but she is a good nurse."

"I'd like to take a shower, and then I'd like to go see my baby," I said.

"Well, I think that can be arranged. After you shower, give me a buzz and I'll have someone go with you to the nursery." The nurse gave me a fresh towel and wash cloth and went into the bathroom and turned the shower on. "I'll see you in a little bit," she said.

"Thanks." I was so excited. I was going to see my baby and nobody was telling me no, you can't see her. This has to be a good sign, I thought to myself.

I was all cleaned up now. My hair was fixed, my makeup was on, and I had on the new housecoat Mother had bought me. I looked pretty good for having just had a baby. When I was ready to go I pressed the buzzer. A young candy-striper came into my room. "Are you ready?" she asked.

"You bet I am, let's go." I couldn't wait to get to the nursery.

"Hey, don't you think you should slow down a little?" the candy-striper said to me.

"Why?" I asked, "I feel fine."

"Well, you are the first mother I've taken to the nursery that wasn't shuffling her feet and walking slower than a turtle. It took me ten minutes once to get a mother to the nursery. I thought we would never get there, so I got a wheelchair while she was looking at her baby and when she was ready to go back to her room, I told her I would take her back in the wheelchair. She thought that was a good idea and I was glad I didn't have to walk her back to her room." She let out a little chuckle and I smiled at her. I was still thinking about her calling me a mother. I *was* a mother. I was the mother of this tiny baby I was about to see.

We got to the nursery window. "My gosh, look at all these babies. Where is my baby?" I asked. I had an urgent sound to my voice. "I'll go see," and the candy-striper left me. A few minutes later a nurse wheeled a baby in a different kind of bed up to the window, and placed the incubator and the baby in it as close to the window as she could. My whole face must have lit up because she gave me a great big smile. She looked almost as happy as I felt. I mouthed the words "thank-you" without using my voice and she turned and walked away. I bent down until I was about at eye level with the baby. She was all bundled up in a light-weight blanket. What a beautiful face! I stood up straight and cocked my head from side to side. I was trying to decide who she looked like, and as I looked at her I saw Mike in that little face.

Her nose looked like a small version of Mike's and her ears were tiny and shaped just like Mike's. I had big ears and my brother and sisters used to tease me awfully. "Hey, Dumbo," they used to call me. Thank you, God, I said to myself, she doesn't have my ears. I started talking to this baby on the other side of the window. "Are you all right? Are they feeding you good? Mama's here. Mama loves you."

Another woman in a house coat came shuffling over to me and stood by me. "Boy or girl?" she asked.

"A girl," I beamed.

"Oh, she's beautiful. She's so tiny though!"

"She was born a month early. She only weighs four pounds thirteen ounces," I said in a sad voice.

"Oh don't you worry" said the woman. "The doctors here are just wonderful. You would be surprised at what they can do nowadays for babies that are born too early. This is my second baby. He's the one next to the wall," she pointed to her baby. "He weighed eight pounds two ounces, almost a pound more than my first. I have two boys now. What a handful!" she laughed. "Well, I'm going back to my room now, your baby is just gorgeous. Don't you worry, she's going to be just fine. See you later," she said, and started shuffling back to her room.

I remained by the window just staring at my baby. She slept all the time I stood there. Oh please wake up and look at me, I thought to myself.

The candy-striper was standing next to me. "I think I had better take you back to your room, you're looking a little wobbly." I was feeling a little weak now.

"I guess I'd better," I said. " 'Bye little one, I'll see you soon. Oh look, look, she's yawning." I tugged on the candy-striper's arm. The baby yawned again and attempted to open her eyes, but she only blinked a few times before closing her eyes and going back to sleep. "She sure is cute," the candy-striper said. "Yes, she is." I was beaming with a wonderful sense of accomplishment. This baby was *mine.* I was her mother and I was experimenting with my first maternal feelings. " 'Bye now, I love you," I said, and waved to the sleeping, unaware baby in her little incubator.

I was walked much more slowly back to the room. "Am I gonna have to get you a wheelchair?" said the candy-striper, and we both started laughing.

I got back into bed and stared out the window. It was a beautiful day. What is today, anyway? April 7th, that's what it is. April 6th, that's the baby's birthday. I picked up a pencil and a piece of paper off the night stand. "Erica," I wrote. Erica what? What will her middle name be, Erica Rebecca? No, that doesn't sound right. I had decided to name her Erica while I was at the home. I don't even think I had thought of any boy's names. "Erica Jayne," I wrote on a piece of paper. That's it. My best friend's middle name is Jayne, Kellee Jayne. That will make her happy, I thought.

There was a tap on the door. "Come in," I said. There stood

Greg with a bouquet of purple flowers. I felt all warm inside when I saw him. "How are you doing, little girl?" He walked over and put the flowers on the night stand and bent over and kissed my forehead. I reached up and put my hands on his face before he could stand back up, and kissed his lips. He sat on the bed next to me and wrapped his arms around me, our lips not leaving each other. His mouth was always so gentle on mine. My hands were still holding his face and I broke the kiss. I patted his cheek and picked up the flowers he had brought. "They're beautiful, thank you," I said.

"You're beautiful, Becki, and so is your baby."

"What? You've seen the baby? When, when did you see the baby?"

"Just a few minutes ago, before I came up here. I went to the nursery and asked which baby was the Rankin baby and the nurse pointed to the baby next to the window." I hope they haven't forgotten about her, I thought to myself. "Anyway," Greg continued, "I just saw her. She looks like you, Becki."

"You really think so?" I asked. She looks just like Mike, I thought to myself, but I would never say that to Greg.

"I called your house this morning and your mom said you had had the baby. Are you all right?"

"I'm just fine, Greg."

"Becki?"

"What, Greg?"

"Will you marry me? I can love the baby, too. She's a part of you and I love you so much."

"I love you, too, Greg. But I can't marry you because you feel sorry for me and you think you are doing the right thing for me and the baby. Listen, Greg. I've been through this before. I wouldn't marry Mike for the same reason I can't marry you. When I do get married it will be because the man loves *me*, not because he feels obliged to marry me. I will never marry a man who would resent me a few years down the road and leave me because the love wasn't there. You know how much I love you, Greg, and no matter what happens in our lives, I will always love you. We can talk about this some other time, all right, Greg?"

His head was lowered, and when he looked up at me, there were tears in his eyes. My heart ached. We held each other until someone knocked on the door.

"May I come in?" A woman came in holding a folder clutched to her chest.

"Yes, come in," I said.

"My name is Sharon Baldwin. I've come to talk to you about your baby." Greg stood up from the bed. "I'll see you later, tonight, after work." Greg kissed my forehead and left.

"Is that the baby's father?" the woman asked.

"No," I said, "the baby's father was drafted, he's in the Marines and I haven't heard from him in months."

"Oh, I see," she said, raising her eyebrows in a questioning manner. "May I sit down?" She pulled the chair close to the bed. "Becki," she began, "I am associated with the Morris's home for unwed mothers. I understand you were in the Morris's home in Washington."

"Yes, I was," I said.

"I had a long talk with your mother this morning. She asked me to come over and talk with you."

I could feel every muscle in my body tense up. Be polite, Becki, respect adults when they are talking to you. Don't you ever be disrespectful to anyone in authority. Words I had been taught growing up and had always tried to follow. I'll listen to her, I thought, but I don't want to.

"First of all, Becki, I would like to ask you some questions about yourself, and then I'd like to ask you some questions about the father of the baby." I answered all her questions about Mike and myself. "After you leave the hospital, what are your plans, Becki?"

"Well," I began, "I would like to finish school and after I graduate I'm going to find a job. I hope to find my own apartment; I don't think Mom will let the baby and me stay with her very long."

"I see," the lady said. "So your plan is to keep your baby?"

"Yes," I said. Why is she looking at me like that, I wondered. I didn't have to wonder very long; she let it go all at once.

"So after you leave the hospital and go back to school, who is going to take care of the baby? Your mother has told me you are not coming home with the baby. Where are you and the baby going to live? You have no job; who is going to pay for your food? The baby has to eat. If you do get a job, who is going to take care of the baby? Your mother is in school and works; she is not going to quit school and quit her job to stay home with the baby. You will have to hire a baby-sitter and after you pay the baby-sitter, with the kind of job you will probably have, there still won't be enough money for the two of you to live on. Your friends will want you to go out with them, but you won't be able to because you will have no one to watch the baby, or you won't be able to afford the baby-sitter. Then you will begin to resent the baby for disrupting your life so much. What about a father for the baby? I understand your father left your mother and your father has been absent. Would you want your baby to grow up without a father? It's very important for a child to have both role models. I don't know if you have thought about this or not, but it is very seldom a man will want to marry or even be involved with a woman who has a child. Have you thought about your child? Suppose you don't marry. When your child goes to school the other children will ask her where her father is, and she will have to tell them she has never had a father. Then she will be labeled 'illegitimate.' Is this what you want your child to go through?

"You are young, Becki, you have your whole life ahead of you, you can go on to college, travel, do what you've always wanted to do. Your baby could be placed in a loving home with both mother and father, with people who want a child and who will love that child dearly. To think you can do what is best for your baby is just your dream; it is not reality. You made a mistake, and we are here to help you correct your mistake."

My jaws ached from clenching my teeth so hard. "Mistake! Mistake! You think my baby is a mistake? She's the best thing that has ever happened to me! And one more thing," I was choking on my words now, "as far as my baby being unwanted, she's not unwanted. She's wanted by me." I laid my face in my hands and couldn't stop crying.

"You are upset, Becki. I'll come back again and we will talk."

"I don't want you to come back," I sobbed.

"Then someone else will come to talk to you." She got up and moved the chair back into the corner and left the room.

I had been so happy only a few minutes ago. I had just seen my baby for the first time, I had just experienced an instant love with someone I had only seen once in my life, and now I was lying on a hard hospital bed wishing I could just stop breathing forever.

The rest of the day continued with several other people coming to my room explaining to me what an "unjust" thing I would be doing to my daughter if I kept her. I took many walks to the nursery to see my baby and to make sure she was still there.

That evening Mom came. We talked and talked and we argued.

"Mom," I said, "you've seen Erica. That's your grandchild! How can you still feel this way?"

"Rebecca, I'm only doing what I feel is best for the baby. You are not prepared to raise a child on your own. You just don't understand what is involved in raising a child, let alone doing it all by yourself."

No more talk, no more listening, just leave me alone; that's all I could think about as Mom continued with her sermon. "I'm tired, Mom, I'm going to go down to the nursery. Do you want to walk down with me?"

"Yes, I'll walk down with you," she said.

It was a silent walk; not even a word. The nurse brought Erica to the window. My heart melted, but there was no change of expression from Mom.

"Mom, isn't she just beautiful?"

"Yes, she is, Rebecca." I'll never change her mind, I thought. "I'm going to go home now. Do you want me to walk you back to your room?"

"No, Mom, I'll stay here for a little while."

"I'll see you tomorrow," she said. As she walked away from me I looked at her. How could she not feel what I feel? Something is not right here. Who has she been talking to, who's telling her to act this way? She's not doing this on her own. I was too tired to even think anymore. "Goodnight, Erica, Mommy will see you in the morning. I love you."

The next morning I had just gotten out of the shower and was sitting on the bed brushing my hair when there was a knock at the door. "Come in," I said. A young woman with long, sandy-colored hair, a pale complexion, and blue jeans on came in.

"Hi, Rebecca, my name is Kathy." As soon as she called me Rebecca I knew my mother was involved with this. I was right. She continued, "I spoke with your mother last night and she asked me if I would come and have a talk with you. Rebecca, I know what you are going through. I was there once. I had a baby when I was sixteen. I thought I knew it all; no one was going to take my baby away from me. My mother let me bring the baby home. That didn't work out very well because I tried to go back to school so I could graduate. The kids at school treated me different, and my girlfriends drifted away from me because I couldn't go do things with them anymore—I had to go home and take care of the baby. My son was sick a lot the first year, and all Mom and I did was fight. I quit school and got a job. My son is six years old now and it's been the hardest six years of my life. If I had to do it all again, I wouldn't have put my son through all the mess I've made of my life. Don't get me wrong, it's not that I don't love my son. I love him more than anyone in this world, but he deserved a much better life than what I had to give him."

"But he has you," I said.

"Yes he does, and that's about all he has. I want so much to give him the toys like his friends have and nice clothes. I want to give him so much, and it hurts when I can't because we don't have the money. You see, Becki, you have a choice to make: you can keep your baby and go through what I've gone through, or you can give your child up for adoption and know she is loved and cared for. I hope you will think about what I have said, Becki. I know this is awfully hard on you, but you have to think about what is best for the baby."

"I'll think about it," I said, and she told me goodbye.

That afternoon a social worker came to my room and I heard the same words all over again. I looked at her as though I were listening to what she was saying, but all I was thinking about was going to the nursery to see Erica.

That evening, just before visiting hours were over, I had another visitor. I sat up in bed and pulled the covers up around me as he walked into the room. It was David Murray, the man from our neighborhood whom I had helped with his insurance company one summer, the man whose kids I had baby-sat, whose home I cleaned once a week, whose house we had bought. I couldn't imagine why he had come to see me: maybe just to be nice, I thought. Maybe he will say congratulations.

"Rebecca, your mother has talked to me several times on the phone, and this evening she came over crying. She says you won't listen to her. She's trying to make you understand how difficult it is to raise a child on your own. Your mother tells me she won't help you if you keep the baby. Where will you go and how will you live? You can't ask your grandmother for any help—I have already talked to her, and she is very much against you keeping the baby. Whether or not I agree with her reasoning doesn't matter now. What matters is that you get on with your life and forget this happened. There is just too much involved in raising a child. You can't raise a child on love. For once in your life, Rebecca, stop thinking about yourself and what *you* want; think about what is best for the baby, not what is best for you. If you love that baby as much as you say you do, then let her be with a family. A child needs a father, Rebecca, even though you don't think so. For once in your life, Rebecca, stop being so selfish, think of your child, and not yourself."

"It is 8:00. Visiting hours are over," a voice came over the intercom.

"Well, I guess I had better be going," said Mr. Murray. "I hope you will really think about what I said, Rebecca."

"I will, Mr. Murray. Thanks for coming. Goodnight."

No more, no more, I give up, I can't take anymore of this, my mind was exploding with, "Stop being so selfish! Do what is right for the baby; you are only thinking about yourself." Was I really, I thought?

I went to the nursery to check on Erica and tell her good-night. Why doesn't she ever cry? Why is she always so peaceful, I thought to myself.

The next morning the doctor came in to see how I was doing. He checked me over and told me I was doing just fine and could leave that afternoon. "What about the baby?" I asked him. "Well, Becki, the baby will be staying here for at least two weeks until she gains a little more weight and gets strong enough to be out of the incubator. Now don't you worry, they're taking very good care of her and you can come and see her every day if you would like. Now, I want to see you a week from today. Call my office in the morning and make your appointment. Do you have any questions?"

"No, Doctor Edwards, thank you for everything."

"You're welcome, Becki. I hope everything turns out the way you want it to."

"Thanks," I said. I called Mom and told her what the doctor had said.

"I'll come pick you up around four o'clock," she said. "See you then."

I spent most of the day at the nursery window. When I first got down to the nursery a man in a suit was standing by Erica's bed. She was off to the side in a separate room from the other babies, but I could see the man and Erica. Now I could see the stethoscope around his neck. He was listening to her chest. Then he rolled her over and put the stethoscope to her back. Then he clapped his hands over the top of her and she reached up with both hands grabbing at air. She was crying now. He scared her, I thought to myself. Was that necessary? My face was pressed so close to the window that my nose was touching the glass. A nurse on the other side of the room caught my eye and I looked at her. She was looking at me and laughing. I guess I must have looked pretty stupid with my face pressed up against the glass. She walked over to the doctor and said something to him. They both looked over at me. The nurse started walking towards me. She came out of the nursery and said, "That is Doctor Johnson. He would like to talk to you after he gets through checking the baby."

The doctor came out of the nursery and introduced himself to me.

"How's the baby doing?" I asked.

"The baby is progressing nicely. She is a little lazy about eating. The nurses have quite a time feeding her because she keeps going back to sleep and they have to keep waking her up until she finishes her bottle."

"Why is she so sleepy all the time?" I asked the doctor.

"Oh, that's normal with preemies, they're just not as alert as full-term babies; nothing to worry about. Her reflexes are good and her hearing is normal. She'll be a lot stronger in a few more weeks. She'll be ready to go home in no time. I'll talk with you again."

I felt relieved when he told me Erica was doing just fine. He was the only person I had talked to in days that wasn't questioning my ability as a mother. I felt good; I was ready to go home now. Erica was safe and I would be back every day to see her. The nurse brought Erica to the window. She was sound asleep again. I guess the doctor hadn't upset her too much. "I'm going home now, Erica, I'll see you tomorrow. You be good now. I love you, sweetie."

Mom was in the room waiting for me. "Where have you been?" she asked.

"I was at the nursery telling Erica good-bye."

She turned and looked at me with a strange expression. "So you've decided to do the right thing; you're finally realizing that what everyone has told you is true?"

"No, Mom," I said, "I was telling Erica goodbye from here, not that I was telling her goodbye forever. Let's go, Mom. I'm ready to go now."

I COULDN'T sleep that night. I wasn't close to Erica, I couldn't just walk down to the nursery whenever I wanted to see her. I thought morning would never come. Mom had left early to go somewhere and my brother Ron was sitting in the living room looking over some school papers. Ron was in college now.

"Ron—"

"What?" he asked.

"Will you take me to the hospital now? I want to go see Erica. Mom's gone and I don't want to wait until she comes home."

"Oh, God, Rebecca. Will you just leave well enough alone? Why are you doing this to yourself? You're not going to keep the baby and you know that! Just stop it, will you?"

"Ron, what's the matter with you? Why did you say that to me?

What's going on, Ron, tell me!" I waited for Ron to say something, but he didn't. "Thank you so much for all your understanding," I said, and opened the hall closet and took my coat out and put it on. "I'm walking to the hospital." I walked out the door.

The door flung open and Ron rushed out.

"What the hell do you think you are doing? You just had a baby and you have no business walking anywhere! Now get back in here. I mean it, Rebecca."

"I'm going to the hospital," I said, "and if you won't take me, I'm walking."

I started walking down the driveway and Ron ran back into the house and grabbed his keys. "All right, all right! I'll take you to the hospital, but I have a ten-forty-five class and I can't be late. Get in the car."

"Thanks, Ron," I said.

I felt a lot better after seeing Erica. She was still there and she was doing fine. That evening Kellee came over and took me to the hospital. Each time I left Erica, I had this strange feeling that I wasn't going to see her again.

The next day Mom told me someone was coming over to see me this afternoon.

"Who's coming?" I asked her.

"She's a social worker," Mom said.

"Mom, please, no more!" I pleaded.

"I promise you won't have to talk to anyone else after this lady, I promise."

I was in my room deciding where I could put a bassinet. I'd have to move my night stand over into the corner and the bassinet would fit nicely next to my bed. The doorbell rang. "Rebecca, someone is here to see you." I walked out into the living room where a woman was sitting on the couch with a folder propped up against her.

"Rebecca, this is JoAnn Turner."

"Hi," I said. Mom excused herself and left the room.

"Becki, I have a few questions I'd like to ask you." First, she asked me about my health, then she asked me what my interests were—what I liked to do for fun, what sports I liked. Then she asked me about Mike. His health, his height, his weight, and then she asked if she could see a picture of him. I went to my room to get a picture of Mike. These are strange questions she's asking me, I thought, but at least she's not telling me I'm only thinking about myself and not the baby. She's not saying I'm selfish. I handed her the picture of Mike and she looked at it—no, she studied it.

"Well, Becki, I have all the information I need."

"What's all this for, anyway?" I asked her.

"We try to match you and the father of the baby as close as we can to the adoptive parents. We wouldn't want to put a baby that has dark hair and brown eyes with a couple who are both blonde and blue-eyed. We try our best to make the child as comparable to the adoptive parents as we can." She stood up and shook my hand, but I remained seated on the couch. I sat on the couch and just stared at Mike's picture and my picture on the coffee table. Somewhere in the back of my mind, I knew I had just consented to her— I was giving up Erica. I didn't feel anything. I went totally blank.

Mom came in and sat on the couch next to me. She picked up my picture and Mike's picture and stared at them, then put them back on the coffee table. "Rebecca. Rebecca." I think I looked at her. "Rebecca, you know this is the best for the baby. You want her to be happy, don't you?"

"Mom, why are you doing this to me? Why won't you help me? I'll do anything you say. I won't ask you to watch Erica; I won't ask you for anything. Grandma! Grandma will help me."

"So, you think Grandma will help you?" she screamed. "Well just get in the car and we'll go to Grandma's and see how much she will help you."

Mom and I drove to Grandma's. I knocked on the door. Grandma opened the door and looked at me. She hadn't seen me since I had told her I was pregnant and she told me to get away from her. Mom was standing next to me and said, "Grandma, Rebecca has something to ask you."

"Come in and sit down," Grandma said.

"Grandma," I stuttered, "you know I had the baby."

"Yes I know," she said, "and if you are here to ask me if I will help you in any way so you can keep the baby, the answer is no. You did this on your own and you are going to have to get out of it on your own. You have no business trying to raise a baby on your own. What will people think?"

"Goodbye, Grandma," I said, and got up and went to the car. Mom came out about five minutes later. She got in the car and we didn't talk anymore.

For the next two days I stayed in my room. I had enough energy for one more battle. I found Mother in bed reading a book. "Mom, I have to talk to you."

"If it's about the baby, I don't want to hear it," she said.

"I'm bringing the baby home, Mom." She threw her book down and screamed, "If you bring the baby home, you will have no home to bring the baby to! You're out, out on your own! I can't seem to get it into your head the responsibilities of raising a child! You just won't listen. That baby needs a mother *and* a father. If you really love her, you will do what is best for her and not what is best for you. You have a court date this Monday at ten o'clock to sign the adoption papers. If you don't go, I've washed my hands of this whole mess!" She started to cry. "I know you love the baby and I know you want her to be with you, but I can't help you this time, Rebecca. I just can't. Someday you will forget this ever happened."

I went back to my room and sat on my bed. I thought about Erica. Where would I take her? How could I pay for her food and clothes? Had I really been thinking of her needs and not just my own? If giving Erica up for adoption was the only way of showing these people who I thought cared about me that I truly did love her and wanted the very best for her and that I wasn't selfish and uncaring—if this was the true meaning of love, I would prove to everyone, including myself, that giving Erica up for adoption was my way of showing her I loved her. I had been defeated. I knew of no other recourse, and no one offered any other alternatives or any hope of any kind.

Monday morning came. Mom was sitting in the chair in the living room reading the morning paper. "Mom," I said, "I have to go to the hospital. I have to see Erica and tell her goodbye, and then I will sign the papers." Mother knew that was a condition I had just made.

"We will have to leave a little early then," she said. "Go get ready."

We didn't talk at all on the way to the hospital. I got out of the car and just looked at Mom and shut the door.

I walked to the nursery window and one of the nurses recognized me and went and got Erica and brought her to the window. I stared at her sleeping, peaceful face. I wanted to hold her, I wanted to kiss her, I wanted to touch her face. No one was around the nursery but me; it wouldn't have mattered anyway.

I began talking to Erica.

"Please wake up, please look at me." She continued to sleep. "I love you, Erica, I will always love you. I will see you again someday. Please be happy. Mommy loves you so much. I have to go now, Erica—please forgive me—I love you—"

The nurse who had brought Erica to me so many times was standing a little ways from Erica's bed. I looked into her eyes. She had a pained expression on her face and tears were streaming down her face, too. A nurse whom I didn't even know but had seen time and time again at the nursery was also crying for me and Erica. I gave her a look of thanks and looked at Erica one last time. I placed my hand on the nursery window and hung my head like a scolded child, then walked slowly to the car.

Mom and I drove to the courthouse. I opened the car door and stood and looked at the building, then looked back into the car.

"Mom, aren't you coming in with me?"

"No, Rebecca. I'll wait for you in the car."

I had never felt so alone and deserted in my life. So many steps to walk up; I started counting them. I looked at the piece of paper Mom had handed me before. Room 107.

I found Room 107. The door was open, and I walked in. A man and a woman were sitting behind a large desk full of papers.

"Are you Rebecca Rankin?" the man asked.

"Yes, I'm Rebecca."

"Please sit down," he said. I was aware of myself sitting in a strange office, two people looking at me, the man talking to me, myself answering yes or no to his questions, but I felt removed from myself.

"Do you understand what I just said, Rebecca?" the man asked me.

"Yes," I said. What *did* he say, I thought. My mind was somewhere else.

"Sign your name here, Rebecca," he pointed to where he wanted me to sign. I signed my name. The lump in my throat choked me. Good, I thought, don't breathe anymore. "That's all we need, Rebecca. Thank you, goodbye."

The man and woman stood up and looked at me. They had no expression on their faces. They left through a side door in the office. I stood up and walked out of the office. The tears were coming so fast, I couldn't see. Somehow I made it down all those steps and to the car. I got in the car. Mom said, "Is it over?" "It's over, Mom."

The reality of what I had just done, of what I had signed in front of two strangers, of losing Erica to adoption, hadn't sunk in. It did not register. I went back to school several days after signing the adoption papers. After my first day back at school I walked into the house, and before I realized what I was doing, I phoned the hospital. "Nursery, please," I said. "Just one moment," said the voice on the other end. "This is nurse so-and-so, can I help you?" "This is Rebecca Rankin calling. I would like to come see my baby. Baby Girl Rankin."

"One moment please." I waited. Another voice came on the line. "Miss Rankin, the baby is no longer in our care, I'm sorry." "Where is she?" I stopped myself. "Thank you." I hung the phone up.

She's gone, Becki, look at what you have done. I was standing by the phone, now I was walking away. I could hear myself breathing and I knew I was alive, but I felt as though I had just died. Not a physical death, but a mental death. I felt nothing, there was nothing there.

I continued going through the motions of existing. I went to school. I ate, I slept. Greg tried to comfort me; even Mom tried to comfort me. I didn't even cry anymore.

The day before my senior prom, I stared blankly at the pretty dress Mom had bought for me. Greg was taking me to the prom. I kept telling him we didn't have to go if he felt funny about it. Several of Greg's friends were taking senior girls to the prom too, so he had no reason to feel funny about taking me.

I hung my dress on the hook on my closet door. I took the long white gloves and put them on top of the dresser. I put my white shoes on the floor, just under the dress. Then I sat in the middle of my bedroom floor. I crossed my legs and just sat there. My dreams as a little girl of dressing up and going to the prom came rushing to my head. But now I didn't want to go to the prom. I didn't want to pretend I was having a good time. I didn't even want to be sitting there. I got up off the floor and went to the kitchen. I opened the fridge and found a six-pack of beer. Must be Ron's, I thought. I took the beer and went back to my room and sat back down in the middle of the floor again. After I drank three cans of beer, I got up and locked my bedroom door. I put the key on my dresser next to my white gloves, and finished the beer.

I could hear Mom now out in the kitchen. She was home from work. I looked at the clock: six-thirty. At seven the beer was all gone. I wasn't feeling anything, and that felt good. All of a sudden, I started to cry. I was thinking of doing something to myself, but it wasn't clear what that was. I knew only that I didn't want to hurt anymore. Did Mom hear me crying? I hoped not.

"Rebecca, what are you doing?" Mom knocked on the door, then tried the doorknob. "Rebecca, open this door! What's the matter?" I couldn't answer her, the words wouldn't come out. "Rebecca, please let me in, let's talk." I choked out the words, "I'm all right, I'll talk to you later." "Rebecca, where's the key to your door?" "I have it in here, I'll talk to you later." I could hear her pacing the floor. I wish she would sit down, I thought.

Half an hour passed, and Mom was knocking on the door again. "Rebecca, if you won't talk to me, I'll call Kellee. You'll talk to her, won't you?"

Five minutes passed, and Kellee was knocking on my bedroom door.

"Becki, are you all right? Becki, open this door, now. I mean it, Becki!" She sounded scared.

As I sat on the floor not answering, I knew I had been thinking about something for quite some time, and it suddenly came clear in my mind. That's what it was, I thought. I became settled with myself. I smiled; I became extremely happy. I started laughing, laughing out loud.

"Becki! I swear to God, if you don't open this door now, I'm going to break it in!" Kellee was angry now. I knew not to mess with Kellee when she was mad.

"Okay, Kellee, listen to me." I walked over to my window and opened it, then went back to the closed door. "Kellee, you and Mom have to promise something: I'm going to put the key on a piece of paper and slide it under the door, but you have to promise me you won't come in for five minutes. I have to pick up some things in my room before you come in. Promise, Kellee, and you, too, Mom?"

"I promise you, Becki. I've never lied to you before, now give me the key."

I put the key on a piece of school paper and slid it partway under the door. Then I went to the window and jumped out.

I had just picked myself up off the ground when Mom and Kellee came running into my room. I started to run, faster than I'd ever run before. Kellee screamed, "She went out the window!" I was on the street now running toward the highway. About two blocks away was the main truck route, the only one leading into town. At this time of night you could count ten to fifteen eighteen-wheelers passing along the highway in an hour's time. I was close to the highway now, and all I could hear in the dark, silent night was the down-shifting of an eighteen-wheeler. Then I heard Kellee scream, "The truck, Becki! Stop! Nooooooo!"

Four hands grabbed my shoulders. Kellee, Mom, and I stood in the darkness and watched the truck go by. I sobbed. "You promised me, you promised me! Why can't anything go right for me? I don't want to hurt anyone anymore, Kellee. I miss Erica so much!"

Kellee was breathing so hard she could barely speak. "Becki, listen to me." I pulled away from her. She grabbed me and held me in line. "Damn you, Becki, just listen to me! You want to see Erica someday?"

"Yes," I said, "I want her now."

"Becki, you can't. Some day you will see her again. But you'll never see her again if you're dead. Is that what you want?"

"No, no, I don't want that," I sobbed.

"Well, you just about made it happen." Kellee still wasn't

breathing right. "Becki, I promise you will see Erica again some-day."

I looked at Kellee and smugly said, "You promised not to come in my room for five minutes, and you lied to me."

"I didn't lie to you, Becki, your mother never promised she would wait five minutes after we got the key." Kellee and I both turned and looked at Mom. She was holding her hands to her chest. I could see her face from the light of the street lamp above us. Fear was all I saw there. Mom couldn't talk.

Kellee pulled me by the arm and told me to get back in the house, where she sat me down on my bed and talked. She made me listen to her. I finally realized that everything she was telling me was true. I never would see Erica again if I was dead. What good was I doing myself? Would this horrible guilt ever go away? "Kellee," I said, "I'm going to try. I'll try to put my life back in order. I have to be strong, don't I, Kellee?"

"Yes, Becki, you have to try."

"I hope these next eighteen years will go by fast," I said.

"Eighteen years?" she said, unsure of what I meant.

"In eighteen years Erica will be an adult, and I'm going to find her." My eyes started to close.

"You old drunk," Kellee said softly, and laid me down in bed and covered me up. I could hear Kellee and Mom talking and I drifted off to sleep.

The next morning I awoke with a splitting headache and the memories of the night before. In a sad sort of way, I still wished my plan had worked out, but then I remembered what Kellee had said: "You won't see her again if you're dead."

I had found a new inner strength, and I was holding on to it. I went to the prom; I even had a good time. I graduated from high school. My life was changing fast.

It had been about three months since Erica was born, and the memory of her overpowered the reality of it all. Mom was so worn out listening to my "what ifs" and "whys" that she told me to go call my Uncle Steve, who worked at an adoption agency. So one night I dialed his home, and Uncle Steve answered the phone.

"Uncle Steve, this is Rebecca."

"Well, how are you doing?" he said.

"I'm not doing very well. I need to talk to you about my baby."

"Go ahead." He sounded curious about what I would say.

I swallowed hard and tried to keep my composure. "I made a mistake, Uncle Steve. I gave my baby up for adoption, and that's not what I wanted to do. I want my baby back. Will you help me? There has to be something I can do, someone I can go to."

Uncle Steve waited for a moment before he spoke. "Rebecca, I know how difficult this must be for you, but there is not anything I or anyone else can do for you. You see, Rebecca, you signed the relinquishment papers, which stated that you had terminated your parental right to your child. Once you sign the papers it is final. I can't help you, and neither can anyone else. Rebecca, you are going to have to forget about the baby and find some comfort in knowing that she has been placed in a loving, good home. I'm sure your baby is happy, Rebecca."

I didn't say anything, I was trying to comprehend what he had just said.

"Rebecca, is there anything else you wanted to ask me?"

"No, Uncle Steve, thank you for talking to me. Goodbye."

I sat in the kitchen by the phone and squeezed my eyes closed as tight as I could and swore I would rip out the eyes of the next person who told me to forget Erica. Do you tell the mother who has just lost her son in the war to forget him? Do you tell the father who has lost his wife and four kids in a house fire to forget them? Do you tell the mother of a child who has been drowned in the family pool to forget it? Uncle Steve's words swam in my head: *You* signed the papers; *You* gave up the rights; *You* have no right where your baby is concerned. I had no one to blame but myself. I would live with what I had done, and pray every day that she would be happy. I would go on with my life, but I'd be damned if I would ever forget.

I got a job working in a restaurant. That kept me busy in the day, and at night I would be with Greg. We continued our relationship as though nothing had happened, but we both had changed. I was moody and withdrawn; Greg was so preoccupied with my feelings that he had hidden his own feelings and hadn't dealt with his own hurt. We tried to help each other—we loved each other—but we were drifting apart.

On the Fourth of July my friends and I went to McCall for the celebration. McCall is a resort town about one hundred miles from home. We went to do some water-skiing and to be part of the crowd of people cruising the main street all night. Greg went to my house and Mom told him I had gone to McCall with my friends. So he found a couple of his friends to ride up with him. He drove around until he found me. My girlfriends and I were sitting on the car watching all the people. I spotted Greg about the same time he saw me and I walked over to meet him. He was angry about something.

"Hi, Greg," I said. "I didn't know you were coming up."

"I wasn't," he snapped, "and you have no business being up here either." Greg took my hand and looked at it. "You don't have my ring on. That says it all." He dropped my hand and walked away from me.

"Greg, wait!" I ran after him. "I washed my car before I came up here, you know I always take the ring off when I wash my car. It's sitting on the kitchen counter. I just forgot to put it back on. Honest, Greg." Greg looked at me and walked away. I had told him the truth, but our relationship ended.

THE MOON CAST ITS
light on the mountainside, and the stars filled the whole sky. They really do twinkle, I thought. If I could just sit here and look at the moon and the stars as they are tonight, if everything could be as calm and unchanging, I'd be happy to stay here the rest of my life. This mountaintop was mine. I used to come here often after we moved from my old hometown. This was my place to be alone with my thoughts. I would drive about fifteen miles out of town and pull off onto a side road and climb my mountain. Sometimes I would go there to straighten out my problems, other times I would just go there to be alone and not think of anything at all. On this particular night I was healing myself. I was licking my wounds. I was tired of my strained relationship with my mother. We couldn't agree on anything; we argued, we grew apart. She continued to make rules for me to live by, and I continued to break them. She threatened to kick me out of the house almost daily, and I certainly hadn't made life easy on her.

I was preparing myself to be out on my own. I wasn't a child anymore. I had left that part of my life behind after I had Erica. I was ready to listen to myself instead of conforming to the wishes of others.

As I gazed at the stars I made a pact with myself. I had failed miserably at motherhood, but I had paid my debt to society. I couldn't take anything back; I had done this on my own. I was the loser. I had been unable to stand my ground with so many against me, but never again would I give in. To belong to one's self is to know one's self. I would never again be put in a position where I would have to meet other people's conditions, nor would I fear the rejection of not conforming. I left my mountain that night knowing I would always be alone when my thoughts would turn toward Erica. Even though the other girls in the Morris's home had to be feeling the same as I was, we were no longer connected with each other, nor would we ever see each other again. I would do my crying alone.

I still thought about Greg and wished we were still together. When I saw his car downtown, I would drive up closer to it; but when the new girl sitting beside him looked my way, I would back off and wish I could melt into the concrete.

I continued to go to my job every day. I went to work one morning and found my boss standing in the kitchen door waving a full-sized apron at me. "Good morning, Becki, I hope you're ready for this," she grinned. Leo, short for Leona, was the boss-lady, short and plump, but with the face of a model. She told me I had been "promoted" from a full-time waitress to the new pudding girl.

"Oh, Leo," I whined, "not the pudding!" "Yes," she snapped as she scooted me into the kitchen. "Now, you put this apron on and I'll show you what to do."

In the kitchen was a long counter filled with empty dessert dishes. "Now watch, Becki!" Leo said as she started with the chocolate pudding. "First, the chocolate pudding, then the vanilla pudding, then the tapioca pudding. After you have filled all the dessert cups, then you put the whipping cream on all but a few; some of the customers don't like whipping cream, you know." Leo shook the can hard and showed me how to put the whipping cream on the pudding in a nice neat rosette. "No spray on the outside of the pudding or on the cup. You have to make it look nice. After the whipping cream is on all the desserts, you put the cherry on top." Leo pulled a jar of maraschino cherries from under the large table and plopped it next to the pudding. "I'll be back in half an hour to see how you're doing," she said, and left me with a can of whipping cream in my hand.

This can't be all that hard, I thought to myself, and let the first pudding have it with my can of whipping cream. Oops. I guess I should have shaken the can before I started, for it sprayed all over five cups of pudding. I'll just set these aside for the waitresses to eat later. Half an hour passed and Leo came back as she promised. I wasn't even halfway through. I had poured all the chocolate, vanilla, and tapioca puddings into the cups and was finishing up with the whipping cream and cherries. Leo stood by me with her face all scrunched up and her eyes closed. She opened one of her eyes and looked me up and down, then looked at the puddings.

"What's the matter, Leo?" I asked.

"Just finish up the puddings and go to the bathroom and see if you can fix yourself up before you come back on the floor. The lunch customers will be coming soon." She walked out shaking her head. After putting on the last cherry, I wiped my hands on the apron. I looked down at the apron and pulled it up to look at it: That's when I noticed my shoes were spotted with chocolate pudding. The apron was splattered with whipping cream, tapioca, chocolate, and vanilla pudding. "How did that get there?" I said aloud. I took the apron off and put it in the sink, then went to the bathroom as Leo had told me. While I washed my hands I looked in the mirror above the sink. My face looked a little like my apron, and there were three small balls of tapioca stuck to one eyebrow. I stood by the sink looking at myself in the mirror. If I had seen this a year ago, I would have laughed like a fool. Instead, I pulled a paper towel out of the dispenser, wet it, and wiped the splatters off my face.

Leo came into the bathroom. "Are you cleaned up, Becki?" she wheezed. She was always out of breath, always hurrying around getting everything just right. "Did you get the tapioca off your eyebrow?" She put her hand on my face and turned my face to give me a final inspection. I felt like crying. I wanted to tell her everything about Erica and have her put her short, fat arms around me and tell me everything would be all right. "Come on, Becki, let's get going. You have people in your section already; can't keep 'em waiting!"

"I'm coming," I said, and followed her out.

After work I went home. I was just inside the door when the phone rang. "Hi, Beck, it's Kel. You want to go out tonight and mess around?"

"Not tonight, Kel," I said. "I'm awful tired. I don't have to work tomorrow though; do you want to go to the park or something? It's Sunday tomorrow, so there should be a lot going on in the park. That is, if you want to."

"Sure, Becki. See you tomorrow."

Mom was calling me now from the kitchen. "Rebecca, could you run to the store for me? I need a few things before I finish supper," she said.

"What do you need?" I asked, as she handed me the money and list.

"Be back in a little bit," I said.

Inside the store it was the same scene, just a different day. Little boys chasing one another up and down the aisles, moms telling their kids, "Put that back," kids wailing, "Pleeeease" until their mothers give in, babies crying. The cries of a baby made me stop and listen. I followed the sound until I found the baby and its mother. The baby was in a baby carrier placed inside the shopping cart. The mother was patting the baby's tummy, trying to comfort the child. I approached the mother and stood by the cart. "Boy or girl?" I asked. "A little girl," the mother replied, beaming. "How old is she?" I asked. "She's three months old. She's such a good baby, she's just hungry now, that's why she's so fussy," the mother said. "She sure is a pretty baby," I said. The mother said thank you and continued with her shopping.

I was thinking about Erica again. She's four months old now. Does her mother pat her tummy and comfort her? Is she as proud of her as the mother in the grocery store? I got the items Mom had asked me to get, but I couldn't quit thinking about Erica's mother. Does she rock Erica to sleep every night? Does she let Erica cry herself to sleep? Does she sing to her, "Hush little baby, don't say a word, Mama's going to buy you a mocking bird." So many questions, and no one to answer any of them. During the drive home from the store I was consumed with thoughts of Erica and her mother. That night in bed, I continued trying to visualize Erica's mother. Was she pretty? How old is she? Does she work? Does she ever think of me? It was so frustrating wanting and needing to know so much about the woman and man who had adopted my baby, but knowing I would never have the answers.

The next morning I called Kellee, then I picked her up and went to the park. People were walking their dogs, couples were lying on the grass soaking up the sun, mothers were pushing their children in the swings. It was a beautiful day for just being lazy. We drove through the park several times, stopping to talk to friends. I parked the car and we got out to sit on the grass and talk.

A few minutes had passed when a friend from school came running over and sat down beside us. "Hey, Becki," Chuck began, "there is this guy that's seen you driving through the park today, and he really wants to meet you."

"Well, where is he?" I asked Chuck.

"He's around here somewhere. If I spot him, I'll tell him where you are. See you guys later," Chuck yelled, as he raced off.

"Well, well," Kellee grinned at me. "Could this be the man of your dreams?"

"I doubt it, Kellee," I said. "The man of my dreams is far down the road and probably lives in France or somewhere like that. I will find him on one of my many travels. I don't plan on settling down for a long time."

Kellee let out a long sigh. "I'll probably just end up marrying Rick someday," Kellee said.

"Well, as long as you're happy, Kel," I said. "Let's go get something to eat."

We were driving through the park to leave when someone yelled, "Becki! Becki! Wait a minute!" I parked the car and Chuck came running over. "Hey, Beck, the guy I was telling you about is sitting over there." Chuck pointed to a picnic table. "Do you want to meet him?" I looked at Kellee and she nodded her head. I parked the car and Kellee, Chuck, and I walked over to the picnic table. Chuck introduced me to Dale. We all talked for awhile, then Kellee asked me to take her home. Dale asked me if I would come back after taking Kellee home, and I decided I would.

I went back to the park and Dale and I sat on the picnic table talking for hours. He was cute. He was big and strong-looking, and had short hair and the most beautiful deep-blue eyes. Dale had the biggest hands I had ever seen. I was looking at his hands and I picked one of them up. "What happened to your finger?" I asked him. It was a little bent and flattened at the tip. He looked at his hand and began telling me how it happened. "When I was seventeen," he said, "I was out in the garage hoisting up an engine. The engine slipped from the chain, my finger got caught in the chain and I was lifted up with my finger stuck in the chain. I was stretching and standing on my toes, and I started yelling for someone. My mom came running out, and as big as I am, she bent over and picked me up on her back so I wouldn't be hanging there. The neighbor heard her yelling and ran over to see what was going on, and he ran to get some other people to help lift the engine down. The bone in my finger is smashed, that's why it looks the way it does." Dale started joking about the incident. He told jokes all night, and made me laugh. We went to get something to eat, and after we ate I drove my car home and he followed in his. We said goodnight at the front door, and he asked if he could call me. I said sure, and said goodnight. I went to my room and tried to remember all of his jokes so I could tell them to my friends at work the next day.

Dale was to be in town for only two weeks for his National Guard duties, then he was going back to Oregon, where he lived and worked in a mechanic's shop. But his plans changed. We saw each other for the two weeks he was here, and Dale and his friend, Doug, decided they wanted to stay here. They found an apartment and jobs and settled in.

One Saturday evening Dale and I went to a party that one of our friends was giving. I was tired that day and the drinks I had at the party made me even more tired. I asked Dale to take me home, and we stopped at his apartment to get my purse, which I had left there. My car keys were in my purse, and I needed to get them that night. I followed Dale into the apartment, but when I saw the bed I fell face first into it. I told Dale I was going to go to sleep, but he shook me. "Come on, Becki, you can't stay here. Your mother will kill me!" "Just let me sleep for a few hours, then I'll go home. Okay, Dale?" I said. "Okay, I'll wake you up in a few hours." Before I drifted off to sleep, I heard Dale lie down on the other bed.

At eight o'clock the next morning we were awakened by Doug coming in the door. I sat up quickly and I could see the sunlight shining on the carpet. We had slept all night; Dale hadn't awakened me.

I jumped up and started shaking Dale. "Dale, wake up," I said. "It's morning! We slept all night!" Dale jumped out of bed and started running around in a sleepy daze. All he could say was, "She's going to kill me, Becki! What am I going to tell your mother?"

"Settle down, Dale," I said. "We'll just tell Mom we fell asleep and that's the truth."

"Obviously," Doug said. "You spend the night with a good-looking girl and I come in and find you both fully dressed and in separate beds, even. I gotta talk to you Dale, you've got this all wrong," Doug grinned, and walked into the bathroom. "Becki, come on, maybe your mother's not up yet," Dale said as he pulled me out to the car.

When we pulled into my driveway we both just sat there and stared at the front lawn. My mom was up all right, and it looked like she had been pretty busy during the night: Everything that belonged to me—old letters written to me from my stay at the home, my clothes, shoes, underwear, the pictures from my wall—absolutely everything except my bed, the night stand, and my dresser was all boxed up and sitting on the front lawn.

"Do you think she's mad?" Dale said. I looked at him and got out of the car. I opened the doors and the trunk of my car and started putting my belongings in my car. Dale helped me, and put some of it in his car. "I'm sorry, Becki," Dale said. "This is all my fault." "No, it isn't your fault, Dale," I said, "this has been coming on quite some time now."

When everything was loaded and I looked at the house, Mom was standing by the window. We looked at each other for a moment, then I got in my car and drove away. I followed Dale to his apartment and put my belongings inside.

Several days later I found a small, one-room, one-bathroom apartment and moved in. I stayed there for a couple of weeks. Kellee was ready to move out of her house, so we went to find an apartment for the two of us. We found a little house for rent and moved in. Kellee and I enjoyed our independence, going where we wanted to, coming home when we wanted to, and having no one to answer to.

Several months after we moved in together, Kellee flew to Hawaii to be with her boyfriend, Rick. Rick was in the service, and he was going to be in Hawaii for a few days on an R&R leave. Kellee flew over to be with him, and they were married in Hawaii.

Kellee was married now. Even though all the plans we had made together were never going to happen, I didn't care. Kellee was happy and that was all that mattered.

One evening Dale and I were alone sitting on the couch. I wanted to talk about Erica. "Dale, I have something I need to tell you about me," I said. "I had a baby girl. She was born in April and I gave her up for adoption." I was crying and Dale put his arms around me.

"I know about the baby," Dale said.

"Who told you?" I asked.

"It doesn't matter who told me, I just wish I had known you then; everything would have been different. I could have loved your baby as much as you do." I felt safe with Dale. I didn't wonder and worry what he was doing all the time like I did when I was with Greg.

It was the beginning of autumn. The trees were changing color and leaves were whirling in the streets. Dale and I had decided to stay at my place that evening: no parties, no dragging Main Street, just a quiet evening to sit in front of the television.

We were sitting on the couch, talking and joking around with one another. "Dale," I said. "What?" he answered. "Will you marry me?"

Dale looked at me and casually said, "Well, it's the least I can do for you, since it was my fault you got kicked out of the house."

We both laughed and didn't say any more about it. The next evening, Dale came over with a dozen red roses and handed them to me. "It's my turn to ask you if you will marry me," he said. I didn't have to think about it very long and I said yes.

The next day we went to the jeweler's and picked out my wedding set. We were engaged, and started making wedding plans. We set our wedding date for November seventh, three weeks away. We had an awful lot to do in the next weeks, but we made it, and we had a wonderful and beautiful wedding.

After the wedding we went over to Mom's, changed our clothes and got our suitcases, and left around ten o'clock that evening to drive to Sun Valley, Idaho, for our honeymoon. We drove most of the night and went straight to the lodge where we planned to stay for the weekend. The lodge was deserted, and there was a big sign posted on the front door. CLOSED FOR REMODELING, WILL RE-OPEN DEC. 25TH. We both looked at each other and I started whining. "I'm hungry, Dale. I'm tired and I'm cold. Now what are we going to do?" Dale looked at me and started laughing. "We've been married one day, and you're nagging me already. I thought that was supposed to come later." I gave him a weak laugh and got back in the car. We drove back to a small town just outside of Sun Valley and found a motel consisting of ten log cabins and stayed there. We spent our wedding night in a cozy little log cabin.

The next morning we talked about what we were going to do with the six days we had left before Dale had to be back at work. We decided to drive to Ogden, Utah, to see my sister, Susan. Susan had just had her first baby a few weeks before and hadn't felt up to coming to our wedding, so we decided to drive to Utah and spend a few days with her, her husband Ace, and their new baby.

When Dale and I arrived Susan was sitting on the couch, holding her baby girl, Lisa. I asked Susan if I could hold the baby, and Susan gave Lisa to me. I held Lisa in my arms and rocked her and held her close. I started to cry and Susan started crying too. "I'm sorry, Becki," she said, and started to take Lisa out of my arms. "Please don't take her, Susan," I said, and I continued to rock Lisa until she fell asleep.

For the next three days I held Lisa and fed her and rocked her. I didn't want to put her down.

Dale and I then decided to go home a few days early. We had a few things to do around our apartment, and I wanted to get started on my thank-you cards to the people who had given us wedding presents. After telling Susan, Ace, and Lisa goodbye, we headed back home to settle down to the married life.

I was pretty quiet, not saying too much, and after a while Dale asked me what I was thinking about. "Well," I began, "when you are seventeen or eighteen, many of the girls are ready to get married, just out of high school, like myself. The girls want to start a family right away and no one thinks anything about it. But if a girl that age discovers she is pregnant and she's not going to marry the father of the baby, then everyone steps in to tell her how wrong she has been and to give up the child. People don't want to see a young unmarried woman with a baby, but a *married* young woman with a baby is acceptable. It doesn't seem right, does it, Dale? Do you think it will ever change?" I asked.

"Things are changing all the time, Becki," Dale said. "Let's change the subject before you get all upset, all right, Becki?" I put my head on his shoulder and went to sleep.

The first year of our marriage went by quickly. Dale and I had decided we wanted to start a family right away. We tried to conceive, but after a year of repeated failure, both of us began to wonder if something was wrong with one of us. We both went to doctors and were reassured that there was no problem with either one of us. We were just trying too hard, my doctor had told me. But I didn't really buy that line. I wasn't fit to be a mother, I thought. God didn't want me to have any more babies. Something had happened when I had Erica, and they weren't telling me. I was beginning to believe I deserved this fate, but several months later a call came from the nurse telling me I was pregnant.

My pregnancy was an easy and enjoyable one. I was two weeks overdue, and my doctor decided to induce labor. The labor began quickly and hard. I was in hard labor for about four hours, and the baby was ready to come. I was wheeled into the delivery room, and I was glad when the nurses didn't put straps around my wrists.

The baby was born with only a few hard pushes. "You have a baby girl, Becki," the doctor said. He held the baby up for me to see. "Just let the nurses have the baby for a few minutes, then we'll give her to you," he said. I couldn't wait to hold her, and no one was taking her away from me. The nurse placed the baby in the crook of my arm. I stroked her cheek and lay there staring at her.

The doctor was talking now. "Becki, I'm putting in some stitches. If you feel anything, let me know," he said. I felt nothing but joy. When the doctor finished he moved himself and his chair over to me and the baby. I looked at him and he had a worried look on his face. He put his face close to the baby, and listened. Then he took his stethoscope and put it on the baby's chest. He called the nurse over to us. "This baby is having trouble breathing," he said to her. "I think one of her lungs hasn't expanded. You know what needs to be done."

The nurse lifted my baby out of my arms and left the room. "I'm sorry, Becki," the doctor said. "I didn't mean to say that in front of you like that, but the baby was having a difficult time. Now don't you worry, this happens sometimes. She's in good hands. Now let me finish up with you, then I'll go check on the baby and come to your room and talk to you."

I was taken to my room. Dale stayed at the nursery. I had been in the room for about forty minutes, but still no one had come to my room. I was starting to panic. I was getting out of bed to go see my baby when Dale came into the room. "What are you doing, Becki?" Dale asked. "I'm going to go see the baby," I said. "Nobody's told me anything." "Becki, I don't want you to see the baby right now," he said. "What's the matter, Dale, what's the matter with the baby?" Dale let out a long sigh. "The baby is going to be all right. Her one lung didn't expand, and they have her in an incubator with oxygen. It's just that they have her hooked to a lot of tubes and my mom and I don't want you to see her like that. The doctor said she should be all right in twenty-four hours or so. We really don't want you to see the baby right now. Promise you will stay in the room until tomorrow?" "I promise, Dale," I said.

I was in a room with three other mothers. During the night, the babies were brought to their mothers to be fed. I would wake up and hear the mothers cooing and loving their babies, and I wanted my baby with me.

The next afternoon the nurse brought my baby in and handed her to me. I was a little scared that I wasn't holding her right, so I laid the baby down on the bed in front of me. "Go ahead," the nurse said, "take her clothes off and check that baby over." I took five minutes removing the baby's T-shirt. "For heaven's sake," the nurse said, "you're not going to break the baby." I finished undressing her and checked her all over, her fingers, her toes, everything. The nurse smiled at me as I looked at her . "See," the nurse said, "your baby is fine. I'll be back in a little while to answer any questions you might have, and I'll show you how to bathe the baby and give you a pamphlet we give to all new mothers. See you later."

Dale and I decided to name the baby Dennell Jo. We would call her Denni. After three days in the hospital, we went home. The first night home with the baby was an exhausting one. We put her bassinet next to our bed and whenever she made the slightest sound or moved so much as an eyebrow, Dale and I would both jump from under the covers, nearly knocking each other out as we hit head on, just to stare into the bassinet. We were so afraid of doing something wrong.

Months went by, and I enjoyed every minute with the baby. Sometimes while I was holding Denni and rocking her, I would start to think about Erica. I continued to think of how things might have been, but I had a method of making myself not think about Erica.

After two years Dale and I decided to have another baby. After almost a year of trying again, I was pregnant. I was almost three months along when one morning I awoke bleeding. Dale took me to the doctor, who gave me a shot to stop the bleeding and told me to go home and go to bed and stay there. I did, but after a week of bleeding and cramping, I passed the placenta. The doctor said there wasn't anything left to do except a D&C and I was instructed to wait at least three months before trying again.

We waited and I was successful with my next pregnancy. Our son was born in 1976. We named him Bryan Dale. Dale was so proud to be a father. He would pack up the kids and take them with him wherever he went. He was so good with them that I wondered at times who was the mother in this family.

Denni was four years old now, and Bryan was a little over two months. One afternoon, while I was sitting reading a book, a strange feeling came over me. It was like a terrible premonition of doom. Something was terribly wrong. I put my book down and went to Bryan's crib. He was sleeping; he was fine. I checked on Denni: she was in her room playing dolls. I went to the phone and called Dale. He was fine, he said. I called my mother, my father, my brother, and my sisters. They were all fine, so this feeling of mine hadn't been anything to do with any of them. What was I feeling? I began to walk the floor. I was wringing my hands and trying to think why I was having this feeling that something was terribly wrong. . . .

Erica. . . . Something was wrong with Erica.

Erica was six years old now. She was in school, I thought. She missed the bus, and was walking back home to tell her mother and someone kidnapped her. She ran in front of a car, the car hit her. She fell playing at school, she's hurt. I imagined all these terrible things that could have happened to her.

The more I imagined the more upset I became. Who do I call? Where can I go? Why was I having these feelings? I was scared for Erica. Something was happening to her and I knew it, but there was nothing I could do. I would have to keep my fear to myself. Whenever I wanted to talk about Erica to my family they would clam up, change the subject, and smooth everything over by saying, "You know you did the right thing."

All I could do for Erica was pray for her. Even though I prayed every night for her happiness, I was praying now for her safety, her health, and her well-being.

"Forget." That word haunted the very core of me. Will I ever be able to forget? Can one really forget? Was I the only woman on the face of this earth that would never let go? For I never would let go. I would never give up on my finding my daughter one day, right or wrong.

The years went by quickly. Dale worked; I stayed home. The kids were busy with school and friends. I was thirty-two years old now. I sat in the family room one evening and looked at my family lying on the floor watching TV. I studied each one carefully and wondered what it was that was missing from this scene. I wanted another child.

Within four months I was pregnant again. I was unusually happy about this pregnancy. This, I knew, was going to be my last child. For several months I felt extremely well. None of the nausea and sleepiness I had felt with the other pregnancies. Just happiness, I thought. You can't feel sick when you're this happy. That made sense to me. One afternoon I was sitting on the living room floor sorting out the "good" baby clothes, seeing what I could use and putting a pile on the side for the has-beens. Feeling a dampness in my underwear, I got up and went to the bathroom. No, not again. Please, not another baby. I was spotting dark blood. Not bright red, and not the same as when I miscarried. I phoned the doctor and talked to the nurse. I told her what was happening, and she reassured me that this happens in pregnancies and that I shouldn't be too alarmed. "I'll give you back to the receptionist and she will make an appointment for you to see the doctor in the morning," the nurse said.

I saw the doctor the next morning. The spotting had stopped. The doctor examined me. "It's too soon to tell much, Becki," the doctor said. "I want you to go over to the hospital now and have a blood test taken. I will call you when I get the results. Now, go home and take it easy. I'll call you later."

I had my blood test taken and I went home to wait. The call came. "Becki," the doctor began, "your blood test is very low. I'll explain it to you when you come in in the morning. I want you to go to the hospital for an ultra-sound in the morning. Come to my office after you are done."

I went in for the ultra-sound, then over to the doctor's office. "The ultra-sound didn't show anything," the doctor said. "It's still too early to tell. A week from today, I want the blood test taken again, and another ultrasound."

"Doctor Larson," I interrupted.

"Yes, Becki," he said, "I know you are going to ask me if the fetus is all right or if you are going to lose the baby. It's just too soon to tell," he said, and patted my shoulder. "I'll see you in a week."

I went the next week for the blood test and ultrasound. Nothing. Nothing to tell me. One week later the same procedure was repeated. I hoped this would be the last ultrasound. Having to drink large quantities of water so my bladder would be full enough to see where the fetus was was quite uncomfortable. I was truly hoping this test would show something. I lay on the table and the nurse said, "Your bladder isn't full enough; I can't get a good reading. Go home and come back in again in the morning, with a full bladder." She left the room. I certainly inconvenienced her this morning, I thought.

The next morning, I went in with a bladder as big as Rhode Island, and lay down on the table. I was glad yesterday's nurse wasn't the one who gave me the ultrasound today. When the test was finished, the nurse told me to stay there; she would be right back in.

A few minutes passed and a man came into the room. He was a doctor and he did another ultrasound. "I'll have the results soon and call your doctor," he said, and gave the nurse a quick glance, the kind of glance that says "follow me."

It took me fifteen minutes to get home and the phone was ringing when I walked in the front door. "Becki, this is Dr. Larson. I have the results from your ultrasound." He was talking slowly. "Are you listening carefully?" he asked. "Yes, I'm listening, what is it?" "You have an ectopic pregnancy, a tubal pregnancy. The fetus is in the fallopian tube, not in the uterus, and I want to do surgery on you this afternoon. I know this is sudden, but I need to do the surgery as soon as possible. Pack what you need for a four- or five-day stay, and come to the hospital as soon as you can. Go to the admitting office; I'll have everything ready for you. Becki, I'm so sorry. I'll see you soon."

When the surgery was over Dr. Larson had been able to save the fallopian tube, but not the fetus.

The doctor and I talked about me trying to conceive again. Dr. Larson said, "You will have to wait at least six months before you and Dale try again; but the chances of you having another tubal pregnancy are fifty-fifty. I would advise against it, myself, but I can't make that decision for you. Just keep it in mind. If you do become pregnant again, you will have to go through the same tests as you did with this pregnancy."

"I understand," I said.

I waited the six months, and before long, I was pregnant again. I took the same tests, and all proved positive. Our daughter was born in October 1985. We named her Tara Rebecca, and she was a loving and happy baby.

My family was now complete. The three years after Tara's birth went by quickly.

THE EIGHTEEN YEARS OF waiting were almost over: it was the middle of March, 1988. Erica would be eighteen years old next month. Even though I had three children of my own and felt raising them had been my ultimate challenge in life, a challenge that had given me great happiness, I had often wondered when my being a selfish and uncaring mother would manifest itself. My family and social workers had deemed me unfit to raise Erica; but now, I was looked upon as a "good mother." The only reason my other children were so readily accepted was that I was now married, and the children had a father. I have since realized how important a father is in the life of a child. I knew the joy of having a child with the man you love, of sharing your love with your child, and the pride and unconditional love one feels for one's children. If those well-meaning people of eighteen years ago had thought me an unfit mother because I had no husband I could not argue the importance of that conviction. Yet never once was I asked, "What do you want? Do you want to raise this child without the support of the child's father?" The answer would have been yes. I had relinquished all rights to be Erica's mother, but nowhere on any piece of paper had I relinquished my right to love her, to care about her, and for years continuously to miss her.

I had always "searched" for Erica. A blond, blue-eyed little girl of two or ten or whatever age Erica was then would always catch my eye. I would search their faces and wonder. If I had just once been able to say to myself, "Becki, you did what was best for Erica;

you gave her so that she would always be fulfilled by the love of adoptive parents," then I would have found peace within myself.

I began pondering all the consequences for everyone involved. Erica's mother and father, and the grief I might cause by disrupting their family, were foremost in my mind. The last thing I ever wanted to do was hurt them in any way. On the other hand, my only want was to see Erica, to put my arms around her and tell her "I love you." She would have a choice to make. She could allow me to be a part of her life, or she could choose never to have anything to do with me. If she chose the latter I would respect her wishes completely and never bother her again. But at least I would have had the chance to see her and tell her I loved her.

Two weeks before Erica's eighteenth birthday I made my first phone call. The first call was to my mother. I wasn't calling for her approval, but to ask for help. I was a grown woman now; I didn't need to be reminded I was doing something wrong. Without an ounce of hesitation, Mother asked me what she could do to help. "Rebecca," she said, "I know the hurt you have had through the years, and I have felt it too. You have never been able to settle within yourself. I knew someday you would want to find Erica and make sure she is all right. What do you want me to do?"

"Mom," I said, "would you call Uncle Steve for me? I know he doesn't work at the adoption agency anymore, but he might know someone I could talk to. If I talk to Uncle Steve myself he will probably tell me there isn't anything he can do and tell me just to forget it. I don't want to hear that now, Mom, so will you call him tonight and get back to me in the morning?"

"I'll call him," Mom said.

"Thanks, Mom."

I had a newspaper clipping tucked safely away in an envelope in my dresser. I went to the dresser and took the envelope out of its safe place. I had cut this piece out of the paper several years back. I knew someday I would be calling this number: ALMA—Adoptees' Liberty Movement Association.

It had taken me several days to think about taking out that phone number. What was I to say? Could I talk about Erica without crying? Maybe they would think I was wrong in wanting to find

Erica. I guess I won't know until I call, I thought. I took a deep breath and dialed the number.

I called ALMA and told my story to Mrs. Beverly Weekes, and asked if she knew of anything that might help me start my search. She suggested I register at the vital statistics unit here in town. "Give them a call," she said, "and they will send you a form to fill out. If you would like me to, I will send you the information you will need to register with ALMA." I told Beverly I would like to join ALMA, and thanked her for her help. "Good luck with your search, and call me again if you need someone to talk to," she said.

I called Vital Statistics and asked to have a form sent to me. What's the next step, I thought. I'll wait until Mom calls Uncle Steve and see if he can offer any suggestions and go from there.

I called Mom first thing the next morning. "Did you get a hold of Uncle Steve?"

"Yes, I did," she said. "He gave me a woman's name who had worked at the agency for years. She has since moved to Idaho Falls. Her name is Karen Poole, and her number is 555-8310."

"Thanks, Mom, I'll call you later after I talk to her."

I called Karen, and we talked for nearly an hour. She asked me everything that I could remember, then she gave me the name of a woman who worked at the Health and Welfare department here in town. I phoned Health and Welfare and asked her if she could find any information on Baby Girl Rankin. She was a compassionate woman, I could hear that in her voice. She told me she would look and see if she had the file and would call me back. I waited for her call.

The next morning she called. "Becki, I have the file here and I can give you some information." I grabbed a piece of paper and pen and sat down at the kitchen table.

"Your child was placed in a home either April or May of 1970," she said. "The parents lived in a small town in Idaho. Both parents were professional people. The adoption was finalized in May of 1971." The adoptive parents had said she was beautiful, very small and well formed. She weighed four pounds thirteen ounces at birth, and was eighteen inches in length. She left the hospital April 20th, weighing five pounds, two ounces. Her parents were very pleased with her. The woman told me Erica had been placed in a very good home and had had no health problems. The family was a very loving family. The woman also noted that the adoptive parents had also adopted other children. She said that was the extent of the information she could give me. I thanked her and asked if I could call her back if I needed to. She said I could, and we said goodbye.

I sat at the kitchen table and looked at the piece of paper in front of me. This woman I had just talked to was the first person to ever say anything to me about Erica. The need to know more was so overpowering, I continued full speed ahead.

Next I called the Morris's home in Washington. After being put on hold for the second time I became impatient. Please just don't let someone else get on the phone and put me on hold again, I said to myself. Finally someone on the other end could help me with my questions. The woman at Morris's told me they no longer had those records from that long ago. The records had been transferred to California. She gave me the address and told me to write to them and ask for the information. I wrote to Morris's, and waited.

Several days later the forms from Vital Statistics and ALMA arrived. I filled out each one with the information I had, and went to the corner store to make copies of both. After I put them in the mail, I felt very hopeful. I imagined something magical would happen. Erica wouldn't be eighteen for another ten days, but I just knew that shortly after she turned eighteen she would fill out the same forms and send them in, and in no time we would be reunited.

The ten days before Erica's birthday were spent writing more letters, making more phone calls, and reading books from ALMA. I couldn't read enough about adoption. I read books on how the adoptee feels, the adoptive parents, and the birth-parents. The insights I gained were invaluable. My biggest interest was in the feeling of the adoptee. Had Erica ever felt like an abandoned child? Did she have hostile feelings toward her birth-parents? Was she even curious about her background or her heritage? When I read stories of adoptees' struggles to fit in, I thought of the tremendous fight the adoptive parents must face. They were the child's parents in the eyes of the law and in every sense of the word, with added burden of knowing that somewhere out there were the child's birth-parents.

On the morning of Erica's eighteenth birthday there was not a cloud in the sky. A beautiful day for a birthday, I thought. But where was Erica? Was she even in the same state? Was she somewhere far away? It didn't matter. When the day comes that we can be together, I have a car, and if it's too far to drive, there is always the airplane.

I busied myself around the house. I kept thinking something wonderful was going to happen today. I had waited for eighteen years. Erica was eighteen today, an adult in the eyes of the law. She was old enough to say yes or no where I was concerned. Every time the phone rang, I jumped to get it. I just knew it would be the Vital Statistics department telling me they had matched Erica and myself. But it never was, so I just found more work to do around the house and tried not to think about it. Yet I couldn't quit thinking about it. Erica's eighteenth birthday. What were her parents giving her? Was she having a big party? I thought of all the wonderful things she must be doing on this special day.

Around two o'clock in the afternoon I was feverishly mopping the kitchen floor when I glanced out the plate glass window. I saw wavy, moving lines. I closed my eyes, then opened them again. The wavy lines were still there. I sat down and rubbed my eyes, and closed them for a few minutes. I opened them again. Still the same. This hadn't happened before. I thought something awful was happening to my eyes. I had had surgery to close the holes in my retinas and I knew I was to call my eye doctor if anything strange happened. I must be going blind, I thought, and what a day to be doing this!

I sat and waited another ten minutes, but nothing changed. I called my eye doctor, but he was busy with a patient. I told the nurse what was happening and she told me it sounded like the beginning of a migraine. "In about twenty minutes or so you should notice the wavy lines have stopped and if you are one of the lucky ones, you won't get the headache and nausea that follow," the nurse said. "What's the cause of it?" I asked. "Sometimes it's food, or stress, or sometimes it just happens for no reason at all," she said.

I hung up the phone and waited for the wavy lines to go away. After about twenty minutes they did, just like the nurse had said. I wasn't one of the lucky ones, though, and I got a headache and nausea that lasted for several days. This migraine must have been my release. I had so much anticipated that something would happen on Erica's eighteenth birthday that when I realized I was being foolish I must have made myself sick.

One afternoon, I was watching the Oprah show, as I did faithfully every day. On this particular day they were talking about adoption. I grabbed a tape and put it in the VCR and sat down to watch. Several adoptees spoke about the need and want to find their birth-parents. Some were still searching, some had found. Then they had three experts talking about the pros and cons of conducting such a search. When the show was over I replayed it again. That night, after everyone was in bed, I watched it yet again. Some of these people were actually in favor of adoptees and their birth-parents being reunited. But one particular guest was completely against it. I chose to ignore his comments and focused instead on the ones who believed that searching was beneficial to both parties. At the end of the show there was a number to call for more information and I called first thing the next morning.

It took about forty-five minutes of continuous dialing before I got through. I was given some information, along with several numbers of search consultants. I had never heard much about them, until then, but I was curious to see if one could help me and I called. One gentleman said he could find my daughter for me for $2,500. I would give him what information I had, he would find her, and I would give him $2,500. I was excited. It didn't matter about the money, I would get it some way, and I would be with Erica in no time. I called Beverly Weekes at ALMA, and told her all about it.

"Becki," Beverly began, "first of all, you know nothing about this man. He may be able to do what he says, but how is he going to do it? What if he goes about it all wrong and ruins any chance you may have to be reunited with Erica? He's obviously doing this just for the money. I must say, Becki, that's an awful lot of money to give to someone. He's playing on your emotions, and I wouldn't trust anyone like that." After listening to Beverly, I trusted what she said. I forgot about the search consultant, but I put his phone number in a safe place just in case.

I was starting to get some responses back from the letters I had written—my booklet from ALMA, letters from the Morris's home. What if Denni or Bryan were to get the mail before I did? Denni and Bryan had never been told about Erica; Tara was just too young to understand any of it. If Denni or Bryan were to get the mail and ask me what this was, I would have to tell them about Erica in a way I hadn't wanted to tell them.

Over the years when Denni would whine, "I wish I had an older sister, a sister older than me," I would cringe and wait until she quit talking about it. Telling my children about Erica was the hardest thing I could ever imagine doing. I failed to do so years ago, fearing that they would be hurt to think that their mother had a life before she married their father. But now the time had come. I was going to tell each one of them alone in their rooms, tonight. I told Dale it was time. He said if I needed him, he would be there for me.

First I went to Denni's room. She was on the phone with her best friend. I asked her to hang up, I had something I needed to tell her. She sat up on her bed and crossed her legs Indian style and said, "What's up?" My first sentence to her was, "Do you remember saying that you always wished you had an older sister?" "Yeah," she said, with a serious face. "What about it?" "You do have an older sister," I said. "What do you mean?" she said softly and looked directly into my eyes. I told her about Erica, how everything had happened, and that I had given her up for adoption. I sat next to my sixteen-year-old daughter and watched as she cried and sobbed. "Why, why, why?" So many whys. I had never seen so much hurt on her face as that night. I comforted her and told her about my search. "Someday we will find your sister, I promise, Denni." I got up off her bed and told her I was going to Bryan's room now. "I'll be back in a little bit," I told her, and left her still crying on her bed.

Next I went to Bryan's room. I asked him to sit down, I had something I needed to tell him. "What's wrong?" he asked, and I told him the whole story. He didn't say one word. After I finished, he jumped off his bed and glared at me. "You gave your own baby away? How could you?" With that, he ran down the stairs. My heart ached. I couldn't talk to him when he was like that. I decided to wait for him to come to me, when he was ready to talk about it, and I went back into Denni's room.

A week passed. Bryan didn't want to look at me, let alone talk to me, he was so angry inside. I was scared; I feared I had ruined something between us. I knew that eventually Bryan would come to me, and finally he wanted to talk. He had a hundred questions to ask, and I answered them all. I could see he had settled this with himself. He perked up and said, "Well, let's find her, I want to see my 'other sister.' Now I have three sisters. Why couldn't you have had a boy? Oh, that's okay," he said. "Sisters are all right, I guess."

The hardest part was over. The kids were okay, and we had kept the lines of communication open. Every day they would ask me about Erica, and every day as Bryan came through the front door, after school, the first words out of his mouth were, "Have you found her yet?"

The booklet from ALMA arrived in early May. I read it through very carefully and derived some ideas from it. I was still reading any book I could find about adoptees, adoptive parents, and birth-parents. One particular sentence stuck in my mind. "Sometimes when the adoptee is searching, they have the birth-father's name first, and contact the birth-father." I had no idea whether Erica might be searching. If she was, and she contacted Mike, how would he respond? Would he deny everything, would he reject Erica? That thought frightened me.

I had to contact Mike and tell him what I was doing. He lived in the same town as I. I phoned a friend who had worked with him several years back. I didn't remember where it was that they had worked together, so I called Kim. I didn't tell her why I was asking about Mike, I just asked her where she used to work. She told me and I waited a few days before I could summon enough courage to call him. I hadn't seen him or talked to him in over eighteen years. We had totally walked out of each other's lives the day I was sent to Washington.

Finally I made the phone call. "Mike?" I said.

"Yes, this is Mike, who's this?"

"Mike, this is Becki, Becki Rankin, do you remember me?" There was a pause on the line. My heart sank; he doesn't remember me. I gave birth to his child and have carried the painful memories of her all these years, and he's going to say, no, I don't remember you! I started to shake; my voice was quivering. "Mike, do you remember?" "Yes, I remember, Becki. How are you?" he asked. "Mike, I'm fine, but I have something very important to talk to you about. When I was pregnant with your child, I was sent away from home. We had a daughter, and she was given up for adoption. She is eighteen years old now, and I am in the process of searching for her. All I'm asking of you, Mike, is that if she should find you first, please don't reject her. She is your daughter, too. I know this is terribly confusing to you after so many years. I'm just asking you to never turn your back on your daughter." Silence. More silence.

"Mike, I'll give you my phone number, call me if you need to. I'll let you go now. Goodbye, Mike."

I sat down and cried. I remembered his voice, his quietness. Floods of memories ran through me. Ten minutes later, the phone rang. "Becki, this is Mike. You really took me by surprise; I really wasn't sure what to say."

"You mean the part where you said, you weren't even sure that was your baby?" I said.

"I guess I've never been sure about that, Becki," he said.

"Well, that doesn't matter now, Mike," I said. "I just wanted you to know what I was doing, and if you are interested, I'll call back and let you know when I find her. Do you want to know?" I asked.

"Yes, I'd like to know," Mike said.

We talked a few more minutes, then Mike had to hang up. After that conversation I stomped and fumed all day. I walked from room to room, muttering, "He wasn't sure that was *his* baby!" I finally decided that if I had gone this far and this many years without him, I wouldn't even think of asking anything from him now. That was settled. I would tell him about her when I found her, but that was it. He would have the ball in his court, and however he decided to play it was his affair.

Throughout the summer of 1988 the kids were busy with their friends, playing and having a good time. Every time I sat down to write a letter to someone about Erica, the kids would ask who I was writing to and how much longer it was going to take before I found her.

The discouraging letters I got back were wearing me down emotionally. The Morris's home was of no help to me. I had written letters and made phone calls for two months, hoping they would have some little piece of information that would help me. Their final answer to me was, "You left the home before the baby was born, so we have nothing on file that could possibly help you in your search." I had waited two months to be told that. The lady to whom I had spoken on the phone so often was nice enough to enclose several pamphlets on searching and groups to write to.

I started making phone calls to the lawyers in town, hoping to find one who would be sympathetic to my cause. I was scolded by some, who said I should leave well enough alone, and pitied by others, who said there was nothing they could do unless I petitioned the court to open the records, but that I would have to have a pretty strong case for any judge to do that for me.

Therefore I stopped calling the lawyers, and started corresponding with a search consultant who was recommended by one of the people I had contacted through my many phone calls. Her name was Sarah Hulmes. In my first letter to her I told her about my search and what I had done so far. A week later, her reply arrived. She explained to me that she was an adoptee herself, and that in her experience most eighteen year olds aren't emotionally mature enough to handle being reunited with their birth-parents.

I was wrong again. I had been told no, no, no, in wanting to keep Erica; and now, when I felt the time was right for us to be reunited, I was being told no, no, no again. I knew I was taking a chance but I felt driven, and I knew I could not give up. I was consumed by the search day and night. I wrote letters, I made phone calls; I did something every day. I spent four evenings at the public library going through microfilms of the legal notices in the newspapers, hoping I would find notice of her adoption there. However slight the chances might be I had to check, just in case. But all I got was eyestrain and a backache.

Next I wrote to the hospital and asked for my medical records and those of the baby's nursery stay. A week and a half later, my medical records arrived. On a separate sheet of paper was written "The nursery records of the baby are kept in a closed file; we cannot give out that information." I examined my own medical records very closely, but I had missed something—something Beverly Weekes pointed out to me. I brought my medical records to an ALMA meeting, hoping Beverly could find something in them that I couldn't. She looked at each page and paused on page three.

"Becki," she said, "there is a reference here to Dr. McNeal."

"What does that mean?" I asked.

"Well, Becki, I don't want you to get upset or think that anything was wrong, but Dr. McNeal is a specialist in handicapped children. I know him. He was the doctor who took care of my son when he was born. My son has cerebral palsy, and Dr. McNeal was his doctor."

I just sat there and stared at her. Erica was handicapped! I had harmed her somehow by going into labor too soon, and felt responsible for it.

"Becki." I stopped thinking and looked at Beverly. "Becki, don't do this to yourself," she said. "This might mean merely that Erica was premature and Dr. McNeal checked her over to make sure everything was all right. You told me you saw a doctor check her in the hospital, and you spoke to him about her, and he said she was doing just fine, right?"

"Right," I said, but as I drove home that night I wasn't convinced. I worried about it all night. I called Shirley Stephens at the Health and Welfare Department the next morning and told her about Dr. McNeal's name appearing on the record, but she told me without hesitation that the child left the hospital a little underweight but very healthy.

Every time I called Mrs. Stephens I became frustrated and discouraged. She had all the information about Erica, but could not release it to me. She was very sympathetic; I could hear in her voice that she wanted me to find Erica. But her hands were tied. She could give me information that was non-identifying, but not more. Still, she convinced me all was well with Erica. At least I wouldn't have to worry about that anymore.

Late one night when everyone was asleep, I felt compelled to start lying and being dishonest in my search. Until then I had been completely candid and very sincere with everyone I talked to, but it wasn't getting me anywhere. What could I possibly do, however dishonest or even illegal, that would give me the name and whereabouts of my child? I lay back in my recliner as far as it would go, put my hands behind my head, and started to fantasize. I thought about my "what ifs" game. What if, I went next door and asked the neighbor to loan me his gun? I loathed guns and there are none in my house. But what if I get his gun, take my three children to the Vital Statistics department, and demand at gunpoint to see Erica's records? I would see Erica's file, learn her name and where she lived. In the meantime, though, the police would have been called, and would burst through the doors holding guns on me and the children. They wouldn't shoot a mother with a baby in her arms and two children standing next to her, would they? I would put the gun down, and go peaceably down to the police station. The children would be left in Dale's care, and I would be sent to jail. But I would get out someday, and when I did I would have Erica's name and address.

What on earth are you thinking, Becki? You're acting like a desperate woman. You're thinking of putting your own children in danger. I shook my head in disbelief. Maybe when you want something badly enough a sort of madness sets in. I'm just tired, I said to myself, and went to bed.

The next morning my dad called. He was driving up from Montana to visit us in a few days. Dad had been married to the "other woman" for about seven years, then they divorced. It was always nice having Dad come visit. He may have left our family to be with the "other woman," but he never stopped loving us or caring about us.

"How's your search coming along?" Dad asked.

"It's slow, Dad, but I'll find her someday," I said.

"I know you will, Becki," he said in a slow, sad voice.

"Dad, let me help you," I said. "When you come to visit, bring all the papers you have on your adoption, and we will go to the Vital Statistics department one more time." Dad had been adopted by Grandma and Grandpa Rankin when he was about three years old. He doesn't remember much of his first three years, except that he had brothers and sisters. He never talked about the adoption, and whenever I asked Grandma about it she simply said, "We don't talk about that," and quickly changed the subject. I had always been curious about my natural grandparents. Did I get my blond hair and high cheek bones from one of them? I always imagined I looked like my grandmother.

When Dad came we sat down and looked at the papers he had. "Dad," I said, "you have everything here in front of you. You have both parents' names and places of birth."

"I know," Dad said, "I've had these for quite some time."

The next morning we went to the Vital Statistics department and asked for his birth-parents' death certificates. Dad was sixty-three years old, so there was not much chance his parents should still be alive. The woman behind the counter left and came back about five minutes later. "I'm sorry," she said, "I can't help you," and started walking away.

"Wait a minute, please," I said. "My father has his parents' names, and where they were born, and personal things about them, yet you can't give us any information?" I snapped.

"His records are sealed," she said, "and I don't have his adoptive parents' permission."

"They're dead," I said sarcastically.

"I can't help you, sorry," she said, and walked away so she wouldn't have to look at my glaring face. "I can't believe this," I said over and over again.

"Becki, let's go," Dad said, and gently tugged on my arm.

Dad stayed only a few days, but planned to come back in a few weeks to stay a little longer. After he left, I started making phone calls. My grandparents' names were Elizabeth and Neal Stanton. I called every Stanton in my home town, and in all the neighboring towns. I called information and asked for all the Stantons in a three-hundred-mile radius. There were very few Stantons listed, but I called them all. Nothing; absolutely nothing. This was going to be harder than I thought. If you have a name, you have everything, or so I thought. Not so. I began to see just how difficult it can be to conduct a search. Even with a name, everything doesn't just fall into place. I put Dad's search on hold until he came back again, when we could try something else.

I was five months into my search now. The summer was almost over, and the kids would soon be back in school. Tara was almost three years old, and would be going to school before I knew it. I had been at home for almost eighteen years, tending to the children's needs and keeping house. I now felt the need to get out of the house and do something different. A friend of mine who worked at a department store told me to go fill out an application there because they were hiring new people. I went in on a Monday, filled out an application, and was called Wednesday to come to work on the following Monday. I asked to work the 5 to 9 shift; that way, when Dale came home, I would leave for work. Tara would be with Dale in the evenings and I wouldn't have to worry about her being with a babysitter all day.

Dad came back to visit and stayed for about a week. I told him about the people I had called, and he asked whether I had called any Stantons in Cedar Falls.

"No, Dad, I didn't," I said, "why?"

"Well, that town was mentioned on one of the pieces of paper," he said.

"Okay, Dad. You're leaving in the morning, and you'll be going through Cedar Falls on your way home. Stop at a service station and look in the phone book. It can't hurt to take a look. Promise?"

"I promise," Dad said.

After Dad left that morning I prayed he would find some information in Cedar Falls. That night when I got home from work, I walked in the front door calling out to Dale. "Has Dad called yet?"

"No, he hasn't," Dale said.

I looked at my watch: it was nine-thirty. Dad should have been home long ago, and he always calls as soon as he gets home. I decided to get undressed and put on my housecoat and then call Dad.

The phone rang shortly after I went into the bathroom. It was Dad. He was happy. Happy about something. "What, Dad? What is is?" I asked.

"I stopped at a service station in Cedar Falls. There were three

Stantons in the phone book. I called the first one and no one was home, so I called the next one. A man answered and I told him who I was, and he said he was my brother! My sister also lives there! We all got together at my brother's house. I also have a brother who lives in Oregon, and a sister who was killed in an automobile accident in 1985, and a brother who died of natural causes. Both of my parents are dead. My mother died still searching for me and my brother Raymond."

"Dad, what do you mean your mother died still searching for you and Raymond?" I was so excited I could hardly breathe.

"Well," he began, "my father left my mother with six kids. She didn't have enough money to care for all six of us, so she took me and Raymond, who's a couple of years older than myself, to the children's home in Boise until she could find a job that would support all six of us. She came back several months later and was told that they put us up for adoption. My sister told me my mother cried all the time. She tried to make them tell her where her two children were. My sister says the people at the children's home figured my mother wouldn't be back to get us. She was too poor to take care of us, so they didn't think she would be back. So that's what happened. My mother continued to search for us until she died. My sister showed me some pictures of my mother and father and all of us kids together. I was three years old, and that was the last picture they had of either Raymond or me.

"Dad," I said, "do you mean these last sixty-three years were all a lie?"

"Apparently so," Dad said.

"Dad, all of these years you thought your mother had abandoned you, and now you find out she went back to get you and your brother and they told her she couldn't have you back? How could this have happened?"

"I don't know how or why," Dad said, "it just happened."

"You grew up an only child, and now you have finally met your brothers and sister. How do you feel knowing them now? Aren't you happy to finally know the truth?"

Dad let out a long sigh and paused for a moment. "Becki," he said, "all I can say is thank you for pushing me the way you did. I wouldn't have found them if you hadn't."

Dad and I talked for quite awhile longer. He told me all about his brothers and sisters and their families. He had finally found the peace within himself he had so wanted all these years.

I called my mother as soon as Dad and I had finished. I knew she would be happy to hear his story. She seemed excited and happy, but sad at the same time. "What is it, Mom?" I asked.

"Rebecca, this is just another one of the Rankin secrets. Your Grandma Rankin could never cope with anyone in her family doing something wrong, something the townspeople would talk about. That's why she excluded your dad from her will. She was ashamed and embarrassed when he left me and married that other woman. You remember your grandmother not talking to your father for years, don't you?"

"Yes, I remember," I said. "Mom, there's more. I want to hear it."

Mom cleared her throat. "Your Aunt Molly, Grandma's sister, told me years ago that the children's home had contacted Grandma and Grandpa and told them that your dad's mother had come back to pick up her boys from the home. They asked Grandma and Grandpa to return their boy, but Grandma and Grandpa said no. Grandpa was a wealthy man and I'm sure the money had something to do with it."

"But, Mother," I said, "all that poor woman wanted was to have her children back, and they told her no. Can you imagine what she must have gone through?"

"Yes, I can, Rebecca," she said. "Grandma and Grandpa loved your dad very much. Grandma never could have her own children, and when they got your dad he was 'their' son, and no one was going to take him away from them. Rebecca . . . your Aunt Molly also told me that Grandma was born out of wedlock and her mother kept her."

My heart raced with anger. "You mean Grandma's mother had her in the late eighteen hundreds, and she kept her? And Grandma shoved me out of her life and disowned me for doing the same thing her own mother did?"

"Yes," Mom said.

"But, Grandma's mother kept her, for God's sake!"

"I know, Rebecca," Mom said, "but Grandma lived by the rules. She was always very strict in doing everything by the book."

"Yes, I remember her 'conditional' love," I snapped. "You do it my way, or you're not part of the family. That's it, isn't it, Mom? That's why you were the way you were to Erica and me, isn't it? I know now, after all these years, how much you were still hurting after Dad left you. I can understand that now. I know my having Erica the way I did was overwhelming to you and you didn't know what was the best thing for me. But you were different to me. You wouldn't help me. Why?"

"Because Grandma thought you and the baby would bring more shame to the family. After the talk and ridicule she went through when your Dad divorced me she didn't want any more talk about us," Mom said.

"Listen, Rebecca," her voice was shaking now. "Things have changed so much in recent years, it just isn't like it used to be. Society just didn't accept young girls raising babies on their own. It's not like it is today. Back then we really thought the best thing for the baby would be adoption. Everyone involved was only thinking about the baby's well-being."

"You all thought I was some kind of a monster, didn't you?" I said defensively.

"No, we didn't," Mom said. "We only thought we were doing what was right for the baby. Rebecca, let's concentrate on finding Erica. I want to know that she is all right just as much as you do."

"I'll talk to you tomorrow, Mom," I said. "Goodnight."

I was hurt and I was angry, but that wasn't going to do me any good now. I had to forgive, or this anger would torture me forever. That night, as I lay in bed, I imagined my mother's face, and my grandmother's face. I forgave them. But I could never forgive myself.

I hoped that staying busy at home and with the kids would help me keep my mind off my search, but it didn't. Nothing did. If I was at home I would write more letters to anyone I thought might help me. At work I looked at every young girl, Erica's age, who came into the store. One girl, I remember very well, came into the store one Saturday afternoon. She was my height, had slightly darker hair than mine, but she had a nose like mine, sort of turned up at the tip. She was with an older woman, and I heard her call the woman "Mom," but the two of them looked absolutely nothing alike. I couldn't help myself; I stared at her and watched her every move. This was my daughter and her mother, I thought to myself. They both know who I am, and they have come here to check me out, to see what I look like. But neither one of them even glanced my way. I watched as they both left the store.

I knew I was going to have to stop this, but how? I found myself turning from a mild-mannered happy wife, mother, and home-maker, into a bumbling, overwrought crazy woman. Why was I so intent upon finding Erica? Why did I think this was something she wanted? A part of my life was never the same after signing the adoption papers; my unhappiness and guilt never went away. When one loses a child to death, it can be the saddest, most hurtful experience imaginable. The grieving parents come to the awful realization that they won't ever see their child again in this life. They go to the cemetery, place flowers on the grave, and weep openly. But, as morbid as it is, they still know where their child is. I never knew Erica's fate. I gave birth to her, I watched her through a plate-glass window, I loved her, and then she was gone. I gave my child to people I had never seen, never talked to, and knew nothing about. The finality of the adoption process takes no account of the birth-mother's feelings. Indeed, no one could know her anguish without experiencing it themself. A birth-mother gives the most precious of gifts—her child—and society expects her to forget and go on with her life as though nothing had happened. That's just not the way it works. Every year on the child's birthday, at Christmas, or on Mother's Day the sadness returns. You kow that *you* signed the adoption papers, *you* relinquished your rights to parent your child, *you* terminated the mother-child relationship, and now *you* should bow out of the child's life forever.

A number of people I met during my search felt that way about me, and they let me know it. One such person was my gynecologist, who delivered my last two children, and had been my doctor for fourteen years. I felt very comfortable with him; I could tell him anything. I made an appointment to see him, hoping he could request Erica's nursery records. Maybe her nursery records wouldn't help me either; but if I didn't try, I'd never know.

I told Dr. Larson about Erica and about my search. The doctor sat on his swivel chair and listened to me until I asked him if he would request Erica's nursery records. He rubbed his chin in thought, then said, "Becki, you gave up your baby for adoption. You should leave it at that. Why would you want to disrupt your daughter's life, not to mention what you could do to her parents." He said I would just open a can of worms. "I really think you should leave well enough alone, Becki. As far as the records are concerned, they are sealed, and I couldn't help you with them anyway."

Dr. Larson stood up and opened the door to leave. "Becki," he said with a very stern face, "at least you didn't choose to have an abortion. You did the right thing by having your child, but, really, you need to go on with your life and let your daughter be." He told me goodbye and walked out of the room.

Scolded again. Why did I always feel like a four-year-old who had just been caught by her mother eating the creme filling out of a whole package of Oreos? I closed my eyes and sat there for a few minutes. Well, Dr. Larson's entitled to his own opinion, I said to myself, and left his office and went home.

That evening I thought about what Dr. Larson had said. I also thought about what the lawyers had said: some of them had felt the same way Dr. Larson had felt. Maybe I *was* wrong in wanting to find Erica. I'll drop the search for now, I thought. If Erica ever wants to know me, she will have to find me herself, but I won't be the intruder.

That resolution lasted about two days; then I was going forward in my search again, more determined than ever.

I had read much about other people's searches. I knew there would be roadblocks and detours along the way, but I was determined to take as many as I had to. I had to follow my own heart this time. I couldn't stop even if I wanted to.

It was now the middle of November, 1988, and my search was at a standstill. I hadn't found any new leads or information that could direct my search. Still, I wasn't as alone in the search as I had once been. Beverly Weekes of ALMA had been talking for several months about her idea to set up a support group for birth-parents. Beverly received many calls from birth-mothers, and although she sympathized with them, she believed other birth-mothers would be more helpful in discussing emotions they were going through. Beverly started referring the birth-mothers who called her to me, and we would talk about the similarities of our cases. I finally had other people to talk to about Erica, and they felt the same way I did.

We started a support group and I named it TABU: The Adoptees and Birth-parents United. I held meetings in my home. We would cry, we would get angry, but, most important, we were finally talking about the children we had relinquished. We had each other to talk to when the frustration of our searches was more than we could handle by ourselves.

I called Shirley Stephens during the latter part of November. I made a two-page list of questions about Erica and her adoptive parents, then went to see her at the Health and Welfare department. Most of the questions I had were non-identifying. I asked how old Erica's parents were when they adopted her, what religion they were, whether they still lived in Idaho, what the ages of their other children were, what kind of work they did, and so on. Some questions Mrs. Stephens could answer and some she couldn't. I told her my whole story: how I had been pressured into giving up Erica, how the adoption had taken place. I also told her how I just "knew" that my mother and grandmother would find a way for me to get out of the mess I had created. Even though I had signed the adoption papers, and they were legal and binding, I had thought Grandma Rankin could "buy" me out of it. Family secrets had been buried before with the Rankin money. I honestly never believed that signing the adoption papers would be as final as it really was.

Mrs. Stephens sat forward in her chair and placed her hands on top of her desk. "Becki," she said, "I don't know if I should be telling you this or not, but your mother wrote me a very long letter several months ago. It was the saddest letter I ever read. She told me you didn't want to give Erica up, and it has tormented you all these years. She also told me how wrapped up she was with herself, trying to mend her own life after your father left her. She said that during your pregnancy and after the baby was born she just wasn't there for you. She said she was a failure as a mother during that time. Your mother has had an awful lot of guilt about the part she played in placing your child for adoption."

"I know she has, Mrs. Stephens," I said, "but Mom's here now. She said she would help me to find Erica in any way. Mrs. Stephens, I know this is an awkward position to put you in. I know your hands are tied, but I just want you to know that I would never intentionally hurt Erica or her family. If, when I find Erica, a reunion is not what she wants, I will back away and do as she wishes. It's just not my nature to hurt anyone in any way."

"I really do hope you find your daughter someday," Mrs. Stephens said as we stood up to say goodbye.

It was the first day of December. I was busy shopping for Christmas presents and trying to get myself into the holiday spirit, but I couldn't. I felt very much as I had when Erica was six years old and I thought something was wrong with her. I would lie in bed and try to sleep, but my mind just wouldn't shut down. I'd start to cry out of sheer frustration. I would have to get out of bed, so as not to wake up Dale with my crying, and I would go to the family room to finish my crying.

On the morning of December 4th, I received a phone call. A young woman introduced herself to me as Joyce Krummes. She told me she had just moved to Boise about two weeks ago from California. She had been involved in a group called Search Finder, and wanted to set up an organization here. She had called a few places in town and my name had been mentioned several times. Joyce asked me about our support group. She told me she was an adoptee and she had found her birth-mother five months earlier. I really perked up then, and asked all sorts of questions. Joyce told me she was a search consultant, and, if I wanted to, I could set up a meeting with her. She gave me her phone number and asked me to call her if I needed to. After talking to Joyce, I felt excited. I just knew something good was going to happen. I talked to Joyce by phone many times over the next few days. I made an appointment to meet with her the next evening.

That same afternoon I got a call from Mrs. Stephens. "Becki," she said, "I've talked to a woman named Joyce Krummes. She is a search consultant, and she may be able to help you. I told Mrs. Stephens I had already talked with Joyce, and thanked her for calling me. Her call reassured me that I wasn't wrong in what I was doing.

The evening before I went to meet with Joyce, I gathered up the letters, medical records, and anything else I thought would be of interest to her. The next evening I went to Joyce's home. I rang the bell, and Joyce answered the door. When I talked to her on the phone I had imagined her to be very short, with dark hair, and a little older than she was. Joyce was about 5'5", slender, with long sandy-blond hair. She was a young mother, and had a little girl about nineteen months old. She introduced me to her husband, then took me to a back room. We sat down and she asked to see the papers I had brought. While she looked over the papers I played with her little girl. Joyce told me about her own search and the searches she had helped with in California. As Joyce and I talked that evening, I began to feel very optimistic about my search. We talked about her fee, and I hired her that night to help me find Erica.

The first stage of the search was to find the county in which the adoption had been finalized. There are forty-four counties in Idaho. I wrote nine letters myself and sent them off. I called Joyce and told her which counties I had written to, and she suggested that she write the remaining counties on her computer. That would take less time than handwriting each letter. Joyce had them typed and sent out within a few days. Then, while we waited for a response from the counties, Joyce continued with further research. My family was excited and very hopeful after I told them that Joyce was going to find Erica. I just knew it was going to happen soon.

Several weeks passed. One by one, the responses from my letters came back. Joyce had put her post-office box as the return address, and she called me every day to read the replies to me.

On the morning of the 21st of December Joyce sounded excited. "Becki," she said, "I have the county where the adoption was finalized, and the case number of the adoption. Now we can really get going on this."

Joyce called me four or five times a day. She told me everything she was doing, and asked me if this or that was what I wanted to do. Joyce also called Mrs. Stephens at the Health and Welfare department and asked her questions. Joyce said Mrs. Stephens seemed to have a personal interest in my case. Even though Mrs. Stephens couldn't tell Joyce anything outright, she could say yes or no to some of Joyce's questions.

I had placed my search in Joyce's hands. Meanwhile I tried with everything I had to have a wonderful Christmas for the kids, but I just couldn't shake the feeling that something was wrong with Erica. This feeling made me more anxious. I *needed* to find Erica. It just wasn't a want anymore, but a real need.

One afternoon Joyce called me with a lead. She had found a name, and thought this girl could be Erica. "What's her name?" I asked.

"Her name is Becky Parsons," Joyce said. I started stammering, "You mean they named her after me?" Joyce told me to settle down. She had some more phone calls to make and she would get right back with me. I walked around the kitchen in a daze and kept saying the name over and over. Then I got really excited. It *must* be her. I told Dale and the kids.

Waiting to hear from Joyce was hard, to say the least, but she finally called late that evening and told me the girl's birthday wasn't right. Joyce could hear the disappointment in my voice and told me to hang in there. I was hanging all right—by one loose thread. My nerves were shot. Every time the phone rang my heart raced. Would it be Joyce? Did she have good news or bad?

The new year came and went. Joyce called every day and told me she thought she was getting closer to finding Erica. But many disappointments and letdowns soon led me to a conclusion I really didn't want to make.

On January the 10th, I lay in bed thinking about the past ten months. Denni had often asked me to do something, or Bryan had asked me to take him somewhere or Tara would crawl up in my lap and want to be loved. All these past months I had told them I was too busy: I was writing letters, going to meetings, waiting for phone calls. I had been too busy to pay attention to their needs. As I lay in bed I remembered all their requests and the disappointment on their faces when I told them I didn't have time. I didn't have time for my own children? I had never been this way to them before. I closed my eyes and started praying. I told the Lord I was sorry I treated the kids the way I did, and that I was going to be different from now on. I placed my search in God's hands that night. I told God I knew he would bring my search to an end when it was time for me to find Erica. I then decided to call Joyce first thing in the morning and tell her I needed to postpone my search for awhile. My search had taken all my time, energy, and thoughts. I had to get back to being a mother to my children. I wasn't going to feel guilty about my kids anymore. I then tried to sleep, but sleep didn't come.

The next morning Denni and Bryan were off to school. Tara was still sleeping. I made a cup of coffee and sat down at the kitchen table. I was thinking about how to tell Joyce that I needed some time away from the search. I needed some normalcy in my life. The phone rang; I just knew it would be Joyce, and I was ready to tell her.

"Hello," I said.

"Becki, this is Mrs. Stephens."

"Good morning, Mrs. Stephens, how are you?" I said.

"Becki," Mrs. Stephens said, "I want you to sit down." I was standing by the phone, so I sat down. My heart was pounding so hard my head started to hurt. "Becki," she began, "your daughter's name is Jennifer Cromwell. She lives in Hawaii. Her parents' names are Brad and Leslie. I just finished talking to Mr. Cromwell this morning. I told him you had been searching for your daughter and I told him about you. Mr. Cromwell asked for your phone number and I gave it to him. He said he was going to call you this morning and talk to you." Mrs. Stephens said that Joyce was so close that she called her lawyer and he advised her to call the Cromwells and talk to them. My whole body was shaking so hard I could hardly hold on to the phone. Mrs. Stephens told me she was happy for me, and that we had better hang up in case Mr. Cromwell was trying to reach me. I thanked her over and over again. After we hung up, I called Dale immediately. The secretary answered and told me Dale wasn't in. My voice was shaking so bad I knew she must think something terrible had happened, so I blurted it all out to her. She told me she would tell Dale as soon as he came in. I called Mother, my sister, and Joyce. I had never been this happy in my whole life. I kept saying her name over and over. Jennifer. Jennifer. She wasn't Erica anymore.

The phone rang. I picked it up and it was Mr. Cromwell. His voice was warm and friendly. First Mr. Cromwell asked me some questions about myself. I told him about my family and myself, and a little about my search. Then I asked how Jennifer was. First he told me what Jennifer looked like. "She's a pretty little girl," Mr. Cromwell said, "she's small, only 5′2″ and 108 pounds. She has long, blond hair, and she's a really neat kid." Mr. Cromwell told me about Jennifer's schooling.

"She's been a straight-A student for the last four years, and she has been on the honor roll." He told me she was interested in photography. I sat and listened as he told me about her, and I wanted to see her so badly. Right then and there. I asked Mr. Cromwell if the phone call they received that morning had upset Jennifer. Mr. Cromwell told me it was six o'clock in the morning when Mrs. Stephens had called, the time difference from Boise to Hawaii being three hours. He continued. "The phone ringing that early woke us all up. Mrs. Stephens told me about you and wanted to know what we wanted to do. While I was talking to Mrs. Stephens, Jenni came out of her room and stood by me and listened. She kept saying "What is it?" After I hung up I told Jenni the call was about her birth-mother." Mr. Cromwell told me that Jenni's face had lit up, and that she had the biggest smile on her face he had ever seen.

Mr. Cromwell told me that Jenni was going through some difficult times. He and his wife were separating. Mr. Cromwell was staying in Hawaii to take care of his coffee-bean farm, and Mrs. Cromwell would be leaving soon to live in Arizona. Jenni was torn between staying with her dad and graduating with the friends she had gone to school with for almost twelve years, and going to Arizona with her mother. Mr. Cromwell and I talked for a little bit longer, and then another line was picked up. It was Mrs. Cromwell. She told me what a surprise this was and how excited Jenni had been that morning. Then Mrs. Cromwell started to cry, and my heart fell to my feet. All I could think of was "Please don't cry, please don't be hurt." But Mrs. Cromwell was crying and thanking me at the same time. She was thanking me for the beautiful daughter they had raised and loved so much. The conversation was very emotional, but it told me how much they both loved Jenni, and that all these years Jenni had truly been loved and cared for by these two people whom I never knew. Mrs. Cromwell told me that Jenni would be calling me as soon as she got home from school, then we said goodbyes.

I had to sit there for a moment and really think about whom I had just talked to. I called my mother and told her about our conversation. I told her Jenni would be calling me this afternoon. Mom said she would come right over and take care of Tara so she wouldn't fuss or want something while I was on the phone with Jenni. I ran upstairs and showered and put on my makeup and fixed my hair. I had to look good when Jenni called. Mom came over, and I sat by the phone.

Dale came home from work. He walked in with a bewildered look on his face and asked what was going on. I told him I had found my daughter: I knew her name, where she lived, and I had already talked with her parents. Dale gave me a big hug and said he had known it would happen someday. "But she lives in Hawaii," I whined. I never thought she would be that far away.

Dale laughed and said, "That doesn't matter, there's always the airplane." I looked at Dale and asked, "Can I go tonight?"

"You talk to Jenni first," Dale said, "and then decide what you're going to do." Dale went back to work, and I sat back down by the phone.

The phone rang. "Hello," I said. "Is this Becki?" she asked. "Yes it is." "This is Jennifer Cromwell," the voice on the other end said. I was hearing my daughter's voice for the first time. There were pauses and silence at first. I wanted to come across as an intelligent human being. I didn't want to start crying, because I knew if I did, I wouldn't stop. I asked her questions about herself and about her schooling. I told her what I looked like. I told her about the space I have between my two front teeth. Jenni said she used to have a big space between her teeth also, but she had braces to correct it. She told me she had a tiny red birthmark on her nose, and I told her my other kids all had small red birthmarks on them, too.

I finally asked the question. "Would it be all right with you if I came to Hawaii to see you?" I told her it would be entirely up to her whether I went or not. "Maybe," I said, "I could come for your graduation." I told her I thought she had graduated last year, and she told me she would have, but when she was six years old she had been very sick, and had started school a year late. I started stammering: "You mean, when you were six years old you were really sick?" I asked. "Yes," she said. "I had all the childhood diseases that year. I was in the hospital with a kidney infection, too." I told Jenni how I had known something was the matter with her. She said that must have been when she was so sick. I really *had* known something was wrong with Jenni! But, how?

Jenni told me about her three brothers. She told me about the sports she was involved in. She was very active, and she sounded happy. I told her it was taking everything I had not to go get on a plane to Hawaii that night. I asked her to discuss it with her parents, and to let me know how everyone felt about it. She told me she would. I gave Jenni my address and asked her to send some pictures of herself and of her family. She said she would do that, and I told her I would send pictures too.

It was time to hang up. I told Jenni I would call real soon. Before we hung up I told Jenni I loved her very much, and I always had. Then we said goodbye.

I went to the family room to tell Mom about our conversation, and Bryan came in. I told him I had just talked to his sister. "When are we going to see her?" he asked. "Well, it's not going to be that easy," I told him. "Jenni lives in Hawaii, and it's not going to be that easy to get over to her." That's when I started thinking about how far away Jenni really was. It didn't matter. I had talked to her. After all these years I finally knew she was alive and well, and that was all that mattered.

Denni came home from school and Dale came home. We talked about Jenni and her family. It was as though a huge weight had been lifted from my family.

That evening, as I sat at the kitchen table writing a letter to Jenni, the phone rang. Dale handed the phone to me.

"Becki, this is Leslie Cromwell. This has been a pretty exciting day for everyone. How are you doing?" she asked.

"I'm just fine, Leslie," I said. "I'm writing a letter to Jenni right now."

"Well, Becki," Leslie began, "I know it is asking an awful lot of you, and if you don't think you can, we will understand, honestly. But I wanted to ask you whether you could come to Hawaii within the next few days. The reason is that Brad and I are separating, as you know, and I'm leaving for Arizona next week. We all talked about it, and I would really like to be here when you come meet Jennifer. I know this is a lot to ask, with the expense and all, but I thought I would talk to you and see what you thought."

"Leslie, I'd love to be able to meet you too," I said. "I'll call the airlines right now and see what I can do, and then I'll call you right back."

"Thank you, Becki," Leslie said. "This really means a lot to me."

"No, thank *you*, Leslie," I said.

"I'll call you in a little bit."

After hanging up the phone I ran into the family room to tell Dale what Leslie had said. "Can I go, Dale, I mean tomorrow? Do we have the money? Is it all right? Will you take care of Tara? Do you want to go? Can I go?"

Dale sat on the couch and watched as I paced back and forth in front of him. "Sit down, will you?" Dale said.

"I can't, Dale. Can I go?"

"Becki, of course you can go," Dale said. "We have the money in savings, so don't worry about that," he said.

"Can I go tomorrow, Dale?" Dale shook his head and started laughing. "It wouldn't matter whether you went tomorrow or the next day. You wouldn't last a week before you went anyway," Dale said.

"What do I do now, Dale?" I asked, still pacing the floor.

"Go call the airlines and ask when is the next flight to Hawaii," Dale said.

I went to the kitchen and put the phone book on the table and opened it to *Airlines.* I was writing numbers on a piece of paper when Denni came into the kitchen crying. She sat down next to me and laid her head on the table and sobbed.

"What is it, Denni?" I asked.

"Mom, please take me. I want to be with you when you meet Jenni. Please, Mom, don't go without me, please."

Dale walked into the kitchen and asked Denni to go to her room for a little bit, he wanted to talk to me. Denni went upstairs still sobbing and crying.

"Listen, Becki," Dale said, "I don't know why Denni feels so strongly about going with you, but she really wants to meet Jenni, it really means a lot to her. The way Denni is feeling now, I don't think you should go without her."

"I've never seen her act this way before either," I said. "I'd be breaking her heart if I didn't take her, wouldn't I, Dale?"

"I really don't think she would ever be able to forgive you if you don't take her. She really does want to be with you and Jenni."

"But what about Bryan?" I asked.

"I'll go talk to Bryan," Dale said, "you just call the airlines."

I called United and asked for their next flight to Hawaii. It would leave at ten o'clock in the morning. That sounded good. I told the lady at the reservation desk that I wanted three tickets for that flight. She asked for the names of the passengers, and I gave her my name, Denni's name, and Mother's name. She told me to be at the airport an hour early, and thanked me for the booking.

I dialed Mom's number. "Mom, I'm going to Hawaii in the morning."

"You're what!" she said.

"I'm going to Hawaii to see Jenni, and you're coming too," I said.

"Rebecca, what did you say?"

"You heard me, get your clothes packed and we'll pick you up around eight-thirty in the morning. Denni is going too." There was a pause on the line.

"Rebecca, do you really want me to go with you?" Mom asked.

"Mom, I really do want you to be there with me when I first see

Jenni. These past eighteen years have been hard on you, too, but that's all in the past now."

"Alright," Mom said, "I'll go start packing now. How many days are we staying?"

"Five days, Mom. I'll call you later. Bye!"

I called Denni downstairs and told her she was going and to go get packed. She let out a happy scream and ran back upstairs to pack. I called Leslie. I told her we would be arriving in Kona around six o'clock the next evening. Leslie thanked me and told me they would be at the airport to meet us.

Think of the happiest day of your whole life and multiply that by a million: that's how I felt.

Denni and I washed and ironed. We finished packing around one-thirty in the morning. I told Denni she'd better try and get some sleep. I knew I wouldn't sleep, but I figured lying on the bed would help me get a little rest. I would sleep on the plane, I told myself.

WE were all up early that morning. Dale left around six-thirty to have coffee with his friends, something he had been doing for the last sixteen years. When he came home he handed me five hundred dollars.

"Where did you get this?" I asked. "From the guys at the cafe," he said. Ray, a good friend of ours, had gone back to his shop to get Dale some more money and brought it back to the cafe. "I just wanted you to have some cash, in case the banks weren't open, or I couldn't get the money this morning, just in case," Dale said.

We left the house a little after eight. We drove to the bank, then over to Mom's, and then to the airport. After getting our tickets we all went and sat by the gate through which we would soon be leaving. When it was time to board the plane I kissed Dale and Bryan, and held Tara close. I had never been away from Tara, not five days, anyway.

We found our seats and sat down and waited for the plane to take off. When it did, I took Denni's hand and held it tight. Denni had never been on an airplane before, and she was a little nervous at first. We landed in San Francisco for a short layover, then we were off for the longest part of the flight.

I looked over at Mom and then at Denni. Mom was reading a book, and Denni was looking out the window at the clouds. I told them I was going to rest my eyes for awhile, but I only wanted to close my eyes and think. It really had been eighteen years since I last saw Jenni. I truly wanted the time to go by quickly, and it actually had. I was thinking of the two times I had been to Hawaii. The first time our whole family took an ocean liner over. We had Dad then. The next time it was without Dad. Mom and Dad had recently divorced, and Mom wanted to take us kids away for awhile, so we flew to Hawaii. We had planned to stay awhile, but we only stayed two weeks. We kids were getting restless, and it really wasn't the same without Dad. I thought about how beautiful Hawaii was, and how Jenni must love living there.

I kept thinking over and over about my conversation with Jenni: her voice, the way she talked, the way she laughed. How is it possible to have such strong feelings about a person you briefly saw as an infant? Even though you knew that child came from you, you still don't know them. I never once doubted I would see Jenni again someday; I just had to. It was all coming true, now. In a few hours I would be face to face with her. The picture of her in my mind as a baby never faded. Soon I would be seeing a young woman. I wasn't nervous about meeting Jenni: all I remember thinking is, please don't let me see any hurt in Jenni's Mom's eyes. I couldn't bear that. This woman who had taken Jenni into her arms and her heart as an infant *was* Jenni's mother, in every sense of the word. If I should see even the slightest hint in Leslie's face that my being there was hurting her, I could never forgive myself. I wasn't going with the idea I was Jenni's mother coming to claim her after all these years. To even think that was total nonsense. Jenni *has* a mother and father and a family she will always be loyal to. My only hope was that in time, Jenni would accept me into her life, and maybe, just maybe, someday she could love me too.

"This is your pilot speaking. We will be landing in Kona in about twenty minutes."

I left my seat and went to the bathroom. I looked at myself in the mirror. Would Jenni think I looked all right? Did I look as she imagined I would? Well, I can't change myself now. I guess I look all right, I thought. I brushed my hair and freshened my lipstick. I sat back down and fastened my seat belt.

The plane was descending. I took Denni's hand and held on tight. We looked at each other and grinned. Mom looked at me. She gave me a look that said, "It's going to be all right," and I smiled at her. The plane came to a stop. All the passengers stood up and stretched. I stood up and started looking around. I hadn't even noticed the other passengers until then. As I looked around the cabin, I counted five or six other women who looked similar to me. I had told Jenni what I looked like; now I was seeing these other women that could be me. They were about 5'4", about 125 pounds, and blond-haired. I was thinking now, I need to get off the plane in a hurry. Jenni will probably think to herself as each of these women get off the plane, is that my birth-mother? But I was wedged in. I couldn't get out any faster.

The line of passengers was moving slowly. I was getting anxious now. I knew that somewhere outside the plane Jenni and her mom and dad were waiting. Our waiting was almost over. All these years would soon be behind us. We were outside the plane; I was walking down the steps.

IT WAS DARK OUTSIDE, warm and humid. I was watching every step I took, until the light from the outside terminal was on us. I could see people standing patiently, waiting for the passengers coming to greet them. I looked around. Not far from where I was were a young girl and woman standing under a bright light. I just knew that was Jenni and Leslie standing there. I lowered my eyes and took a deep breath, and walked toward them. As I got closer to them I looked up. The light shining on these two people was soft and bright. It showered over both of them. I could see no other people, just the young girl and the woman. I walked closer to them and stopped. I looked directly into Jenni's face. Jenni moved toward me, and I went to meet her. Jenni placed a lei around my neck. I put my arms around her and she put her arms around me. Every nerve, every muscle in my body was shaking. I held her close and kissed her cheek. We both stepped back a few inches and looked into each other's eyes. Jenni raised her hand and placed it on my cheek. We held each other again. As I held her the ache in my heart and the weight of all those years lifted from me. Leslie came to me and put her arms around me, and we held onto one another. Then Jenni and my mom hugged each other and Jenni and Denni hugged each other. We were all wiping our eyes.

I became aware of a camera clicking and I could see the flashes. A man was standing in the background taking pictures of us. I looked at him and he walked over to us. "Becki, I'm Brad Cromwell," he said. Mr. Cromwell put his arms around me and I hugged him. Mr. Cromwell was the type of man you could just say hello to, and instantly like. Just a few words from him left you with the feeling that he thought no one in this world is truly bad, just misunderstood. I could hear Leslie talking and I turned my head to look at her. She was more lovely than I had ever expected. By her actions and the way she talked, she was a people's person. I liked her instantly.

Then I was focused on Jenni. She was beautiful, and I could see much of Mike in her face. She had long blond hair almost to her waist. Her eyes were like mine, a bluish-green color, and she had a wonderful smile. Her build was like mine when I was eighteen years old. I couldn't get enough of looking at her. I felt the same way I did the first time I looked at her through the nursery window.

Brad Cromwell took more pictures of us, then we gathered up our suitcases and followed to their car. As we drove, we talked about our flight and about where we would be staying. Brad and Leslie had rented a condominium for us, and apologized for not being able to have us stay with them. Their new home was in the process of being built, and Leslie said she was in quite a mess with packing her belongings and getting ready to leave for Arizona. Brad and Leslie talked very openly about their separation, not with bitterness and resentfulness.

We arrived at the condo and we all took the suitcases upstairs. After putting our suitcases in the bedroom, Denni, Mom, and I went into the kitchen. Brad had gone down to the car and had brought up a pan of lasagna Leslie had prepared that day. Jenni made a salad, and we all gathered around to help. Within an hour we were all talking and laughing. It felt like being with family you hadn't seen in years, and catching up on what the others had been doing.

Jenni presented me with an album that she had put together that day. Inside were pictures of her when she was a baby, on her first birthday, and as she was growing up. I looked through the album many times, then I gave Jenni pictures of my family. She smiled as she looked through them.

It was getting late, and Brad and Leslie were getting ready to go home. I wasn't ready for Jenni to leave, but I really couldn't say anything. "We'll see you tomorrow, Jen," Brad said, and gave her a hug. Leslie gave Jenni a hug and she came over to me and gave me a hug, too. "We'll see you guys tomorrow, sleep well," Leslie said, and out the door they went.

I turned to Jenni. "Are you staying with us?" I asked. "Sure," she said grinning. Jenni had planned all along to stay with us, and I thought that was awfully brave of her, not knowing what kind of people we were, or whether she would even like us. Jenni and I talked for awhile, and I could tell she was getting tired. Denni and Jenni pulled out the hide-a-bed in the living room and crawled in and went to sleep. Jenni had to go to school the next day and she asked Denni to go with her. I went out on the balcony and sat down at the table. The night was cool, but it felt good being there. I sat in the chair for hours watching Jenni and Denni sleep. I looked through the albums one more time and looked at my watch. It was one o'clock their time, four o'clock Boise time. I wasn't even tired. I could have stayed there all night watching Jenni sleep. I finally decided to get some sleep; I could look at Jenni all day tomorrow.

In the early afternoon Jenni and Denni came back from school. They walked in the door laughing about what had taken place at school. Denni was telling me that Jenni introduced her as her sister. Jenni's friends said, "Sure, right, you bet," and walked on thinking Jenni was kidding them.

That afternoon we went downtown to look at the novelty shops and to buy T-shirts for Bryan and Tara.

Back at the condo we sat and relaxed. Jenni showed me some more pictures and we talked about her schooling. Brad and Leslie came that evening with another wonderful meal. After dinner, Brad and Leslie talked about Jenni's childhood, and of their three sons. All of their children had been adopted. They talked so openly and freely with us that I couldn't have felt more comfortable if they had been my own family. Before Brad and Leslie left to go home that evening, Leslie asked us if we would attend a luncheon with her the following afternoon. Her close friends were giving her a farewell luncheon before she left the island. We told her we would love to go.

Jenni and I stayed up a little later than Mom and Denni. We talked about the circumstances surrounding her adoption. I remember how difficult it was talking about it, let alone talking about it with Jenni. I was getting upset, and Jenni must have sensed it, because she said we had better get to bed. I went to bed that night and slept better than I had in eighteen years.

That afternoon we went to the luncheon. Leslie's friends had come together this afternoon to wish their best, and to let Leslie know how much they were going to miss her. Leslie's friends welcomed Mom, Denni and myself like we were old friends. The ladies were all warm and friendly. I was asked about my search for Jenni, and the women seemed so sincere when they told me they were happy for the both of us.

We left the luncheon and Jenni drove us to her house. The house was big and open. There was no glass in any of the windows, and no screens, just wide-open columns all around the house. Jenni took me to her room and then we went outside. We talked about what was involved in taking care of a coffee bean farm. Back inside, we talked for several hours more. Mom was getting a little tired, so Jenni said she would take us back to the condo. As we were leaving, there by the front door were some of Leslie's belongings ready to send to Arizona. I felt so sad for Brad and Leslie. They had been married for twenty-eight years, and there by their front door sat the reminder that this marriage was coming to an end. In a few days Jenni's birth-mother was leaving and going home, and a few days after that her adoptive mother was leaving for Arizona. This had to have been awfully hard on Jenni. I felt so sad for her.

The next few days flew by. The evening before we were to leave, Jenni and I went out on the balcony after Denni and Mom went to sleep. Jenni asked me about her birth-father. I told her about Mike. Some of her facial expressions reminded me of him. Jenni was really quiet for a moment and she looked at me.

"Did you have a very nice Christmas, I mean last Christmas?" she asked.

"No, Jenni, I really didn't. I couldn't quit thinking about you. I kept thinking something was wrong with you. Why do you ask?"

"Last Christmas was the worst I had ever had," she said.

"Why, Jenni? What happened?"

"Well, I'd lost three really close friends of mine. One committed suicide and one was killed in a car accident. Shortly after my friend died in the car accident, the friend of the friend who killed himself killed himself too. I've never felt so down and depressed as I did then. I really wasn't sure I wanted to live any more either."

"Oh God, Jenni, please don't ever say that. I know how much you hurt over losing your friends, but life is so precious, and we're only given this one chance. Were you really having those thoughts, Jenni?"

"Yes, I was," she said, "and it kinda scared me."

"I can't explain it, Jenni, it kind of scares me too. But through the years I have felt something, sensed something; I don't know what it is, but I just knew when something was wrong with you. That's why I had to find you. I could have waited until you were older, or let you find me. But deep down inside something was telling me I had to find you, *now*. Jenni, I put my search for you in God's hands, and I knew that when it was time to meet, it would be because it was meant to be. It *was* meant to be," I said.

Jenni and I looked at each other for a moment and we smiled at each other. "We'd better get to bed now, Jenni, you look awfully tired," I said.

We were to go home the next day. I lay in bed that night and thought of reasons and excuses as to why I should stay. I wasn't ready to leave Jenni, nor did I want to, but I had wonderful memories of spending five days with her and her parents.

We packed and got ready to go to the airport. Brad couldn't come to the airport, so we had told him goodbye earlier. Leslie took some more pictures of Jenni and myself, then it was time to board the plane. I held Jenni and kissed her goodbye. I put my arms around Leslie. This woman was the most understanding, loving, and kind person I think I have ever met. I knew I was going to miss her, too. One last hug and kiss and Mom, Denni, and I were heading for the plane.

As the plane flew over the ocean, I knew I would never be the same person again. No more sleepless nights, no more walking the floor at night, no more crying over the child I had surrendered at birth. No more blame and no more guilt. I had found the missing part of me.

THE PAST EIGHTEEN
years did indeed go by quickly. They were years spent with much
difficulty, but not in raising my three other children, or my life in
general, for my family life has been most rewarding and fulfilling. It
was a life filled with hope, pride, and accomplishment. The difficulty came in not knowing the fate of my first-born child.

I will always think back and wonder how my life and how
Jenni's would have been if we had not been separated. But the
"what if" games are over now. The hurt, the resentment, the guilt is
behind me. This took years, many years, wishing someone out there
could wave a magic wand and say, "Becki, your child is healthy and
happy, her parents love her, she is all right, she is happy." If I at
least could have had that these past eighteen years, I would have had
something to hang on to. Instead, you give birth, you see the
wonder of it all, and, with the signing of your name, your child is
gone. You are expected to step out of your child's life, never to be
heard from again.

With many other women I have talked to this past year, we have
shared stories. The similarities are concurrent as to how adoption
was handled twenty years, thirty years ago. The young women who
were pregnant were not counseled. We were not given options. It
seemed family and social pressures put on the unwed mothers-to-be
were the hardest to deal with. Many birth-mothers believe the
choice they made was the right choice for their child, although the
memories of their baby, their birthdays, certain occasions, never let
the memory of their child leave them. Many birth-mothers always

wonder: is my child all right, who does he/she look like, does he/she ever think of me?

I was one who just never felt "right" in relinquishing my daughter. I was never given a choice. I was young and inexperienced in such a difficult circumstance. As I look back now, it was not the norm or readily accepted to raise a child fatherless. Society frowned on such happenings, society truly believed you had just made a mistake, you had been caught doing something wrong. After giving up your child for adoption, you would forget and go on, continue your life as if it hadn't happened at all. Mistakes we all make.

Today, the placing of a child for adoption is a different process altogether. Counseling begins as soon as a woman decides to place her child for adoption. She is given options and choices to make of her own free will. As of yesteryear, these options and choices just were not given. Today, some young women are still pressured by family members, as they were years ago, to relinquish their child, but the social stigma of being a single parent and raising a child on their own, is not as prevalent. There are many more options for a young woman today facing the raising of her child without a father. I am not speaking of abortion. Nineteen years ago that word alone saddened me, and today it still saddens me. I may have given up Jenni for adoption, and cried for her and missed her terribly, but to look back on that now, I would have done the same a hundred times over, and I would have been willing to go through life, with the hopes of one day seeing her again, than to have never had that chance at all. For that, I did right by Jenni.

As far as options go, there is open adoption: the birth-mother and the adoptive parents know of one another. Pictures of the child can be sent to the birth-mother, letters can be exchanged by both parties. The birth-mother knows her child is well and loved, and can be placed in a home of her choosing. The birth-mother is not excluded from the child's life completely. This I feel can be only beneficial to all parties concerned. I am basing this on discussions I have had with other birth-mothers who chose open adoption. I in no way want to leave the impression that I don't believe the adoptive parents are in every sense of the word the child's parents, the child's legal parents, the child's family in every way. But I strongly believe a birth-mother, even though she terminates her right to parent her child, and knows the adoptive parents are legally the child's parents, to totally abandon and forget that the birth-mother ever existed, to me, is insensitive to her feelings. Birth-mothers have time and again reached out—reached out to agencies that handled the adoption, lawyers who handled the adoption, only to be told we can't help you, you shouldn't even be asking.

Were you one who was pressured into relinquishing your child at a time you were most vulnerable, confused, just not knowing which way to turn? Some birth-mothers who relinquished their child were not pressured by family or social workers into signing the adoption papers. Some felt absolutely positive and assured that their child would, and could, have only benefited from being placed for adoption. To know deep inside your own heart that your child was being placed in a stable, loving, and wanting environment could be only the very best solution for your child. Many loving and happy relationships between adoptee and adoptive parents are apparent. I have seen them time and time again. What a wonderful thought it would be to know how happy and content your child feels with his/her adoptive parents, and how wonderful it would be to know how much love, pride, and fulfillment the adoptive parents feel toward the child you relinquished through adoption. This is when adoption is a wonderful alternative. When a birth-mother releases her child for adoption, she has made a choice—a choice to parent or not to parent her child. The birth-mother who wanted only the best possible life for her child will opt for adoption if at that time she is not financially able or mentally able, or has no support system behind her. A feeling of desperation sets in when the birth-mother is faced with the decision: What is the best I can do for my child? If adoption is the best she could have done at the time and under the conditions that she was in—then she did what was best for the child.

Although the adoptee was never consulted in the decision that was made on his/her life as far as being labeled "adopted," I believe his/her rights should be taken into great consideration. Many adoptees fear that they were "rejected" by their birth-parents. But I still maintain you were not rejected, we chose to give you life. The choice made after your birth was a choice of love, not a choice of rejection. The rejection process continues today through our court system. I instigated the search for Jenni, she did not want to search for me. Jenni felt that I was probably married with other children and she was afraid of disrupting my life. She feared I would reject her. When an adoptee or a birth-parent reaches the time in their life (usually when the adoptee has reached the legal age), a strong sense on both sides of wanting to know sets in. When this want and sometimes a need sets in, the adoptee, and more often now the birth-mother, and sometimes the birth-father, begins the searching process. Many adoptees and birth-parents begin their searches by registering through local or nationwide registries. Some are reunited within days of signing with the registries. Some go on year after year, hoping for a match. Some conduct their search all on their own, some hire search consultants, such as I did; some go through the court system to ask for help. Whether the adoptee is twenty or fifty, their files are sealed—sealed with the promise of secrecy. What do we do for the ones who do not wish to keep their "secrets" from one another?

I will leave this section as it is, and move on to the conclusion of our reunion; as long as I can say, from the very depth of my heart and soul, that I believe very strongly that the 4.5 million adoptees in the United States today would in some way benefit from knowing their background, their origin, their beginning. A national registry could do this. If an adoptee was searching, the registry would contact the birth-mother/birth-father; if a reunion is indicated, both parties are reunited. No more spending endless hours going through old newspapers, more letters than you have ever written, or will write in your lifetime, to places that can't or won't help you. No more private investigators, no more hundreds or thousands of dollars spent on a search. Every adoptee should have the very same rights us "unadopted" citizens have. Whether "good" or "bad," a chance in life we all face—but give the adopted person a "chance" to know. Good or bad.

The year since our reunion has been a joyous one. For weeks after being reunited with Jenni, her pictures were shown to family and friends. I would share our story with "everyone." It was like having a new baby. You are proud and happy and want to share your happiness with everyone you meet.

I had Jenni's pictures in her album she had put together for me, and had given to me in Hawaii. We also had our first conversation on the phone. Jenni's dad had recorded the first time we had talked to one another and given me a tape of it. I listen to that tape often, just to hear Jenni's voice. I know her voice and her face now. No more wondering if she is happy and healthy.

Many happy occasions have taken place since our reunion. Shortly after we left Hawaii, Jenni and her boyfriend, Paul, were engaged. Jenni graduated from high school. Sending Jenni a graduation card and present was something I had only dreamed of.

Jenni and Paul moved to San Diego shortly after graduation. Paul was originally from San Diego, but would go back to Hawaii to surf and after meeting Jenni, stayed to be with her. In June 1989, Jenni and Paul were married. The wedding was held in Scottsdale, Arizona, where Jenni's mother, Leslie, now lives. Dale, the children, and I drove to Arizona to be with Jenni and Paul on their wedding day. My mother and sister Susan flew over for the wedding.

Jenni's aunt and uncle held the wedding in their home. Jenni, of course, was the most beautiful bride I had ever seen. Leslie and I helped Jenni get ready for the wedding, a wonderful occasion I had thought I would never see.

My family met Jenni's grandmother and grandfather, Brad's father, Jenni's brothers, her aunts, her uncles, her cousins, and friends of the family. This family was as warm and kind to my family as Leslie and Brad were to us in Hawaii.

In August, Jenni flew to Boise and stayed with my family for ten days. At night before I went to bed, I would look up at the top of the stairs. In the room to the left was Jenni, my daughter. All of my children, asleep. I would smile and go to bed, and wish morning would come fast so I could greet Jenni first thing in the morning.

Jenni and I talked, we laughed, we got to know one another better, there seemed to be an understanding of one another. Jenni and I sat on the couch one evening talking, Jenni asked me a few questions about her birth-father. I answered Jenni's questions about Mike and waited to hear her say she would like to meet him since she was in Boise. She never asked. I did not instigate a meeting between her and Mike. I can't help Jenni and Mike where their relationship is concerned. After returning from Hawaii, I called Mike and told him about Jenni. I took pictures of her to his place of work and handed them to him. He sat in his chair and looked through the pictures and smiled. I have called him on several occasions to tell him of Jenni and Paul's marriage and how Jenni was doing. I cannot read Mike's mind. I have no idea what his feelings are. Almost twenty years ago, we were talking of marriage, we cared about one another and then we were separated. We were pulled away from one another. Mike's feelings were not considered at that time. He was the father of our child, yet he was not consulted in any decisions made about his unborn child. For this, I feel deep regret and remorse for how the situation was handled, as far as Mike was concerned.

Jenni had revealed to me that she would have never searched for us, the fear of rejection was too great. This I feel is Jenni's way of telling me she would like to have contact with Mike, she would like to meet her birth-father, she would like to have a relationship with him, but the first contact with each other must come from Mike. This way, Jenni need not fear rejection. I believe a strong and wonderful relationship will someday develop between Jenni and Mike. I cannot make this happen, only Jenni and Mike can.

In October Leslie was remarried. Leslie was reunited with a gentleman she had dated in high school. They fell in love all over again. Leslie's husband's name is Phil. We first met Phil at Jenni's wedding. This couple is as happy as any two people I have ever seen. Leslie is happy again. To know Jenni's mother is to love her. Leslie and I share a common bond. I see Leslie as Jenni's mother. A loving mother. A mother who loves her daughter and a mother who loves her sons. The mother of my daughter. The mother who kissed away Jenni's tears, held her when she was sick, sang to her, tucked her safely in bed at night, and loved her unconditionally.

On December the 7th, Paul's parents, Brad, Leslie, Mike, and myself became grandparents. Our grandson, Jace Matthew, was born. I flew to San Diego in January 1990. I spent five days with Paul, Jenni, and Jace. I never held Jenni as a baby, but I held and cuddled Jenni's son. My grandson, a hefty, healthy, round-faced, handsome little bundle with a crop of dark hair that sits on his head like a rooster comb.

Jenni and Paul have always planned on moving back to Hawaii. Missing the tranquility of Hawaii, the ocean, the waves, Jenni, Jace and Paul moved back to Hawaii the first of February.

I may have a little farther to go, to be with my daughter, my son-in-law and grandson, but the distance between us now is only in miles, not in the separation of adoption.

▲

Progress.

Over the last twenty years we've all seen a lot of changes. Years ago, at the time when the events described in this book began, the very word "adoption" was taboo, and adoptees and their families were made to feel somehow "different." Society told us we shouldn't think or talk about our birthparents or children. Children suppressed their thoughts of the people who brought them into the world; parents suppressed their urge to know the people who had taken their children into their lives; both suppressed the insistent desire to know if there was another human being somewhere who looked and talked like themselves.

Nowadays, however, we are more honest about the adoption process, and more understanding of people on all sides of the adoption triangle. We see programs on television about adoption. We read about it in books, magazines, and newspapers. Most important, we can talk about it aloud. Finally, the general public is coming to understand the adoption process, and those involved can make known their needs for further change.

I can remember being ashamed to admit I had given up my daughter for adoption. Today, however, when I mention this—and I often do—there is always someone else to say, "I, too . . . I, too, gave up my child; I, too, am an adoptee."

Progress.